PRAISE FOR *READ THIS TO GE*

"Blair Imani is the teacher I wish I'd had at school, and
now. *Read This to Get Smarter* is a book the world sore]
that blends deep learning with ease and approachab....,, ...
so many of us are asking ourselves. This book helps plug the gaps of understanding that so
many of us have and supports us in becoming better human beings and better ancestors."
– LAYLA F. SAAD, AUTHOR OF *ME AND WHITE SUPREMACY*

"As a young educator at Planned Parenthood, Blair Imani demonstrated her passion for
teaching and building community. In *Read This to Get Smarter*, Blair provides a roadmap to
better understanding the most important issues in our culture today, including race, class,
gender, and disability. She approaches these important topics with humility and provides
readers with the tools they need to get smarter."
– CECILE RICHARDS, FORMER PRESIDENT, PLANNED PARENTHOOD FEDERATION OF AMERICA

"Blair Imani writes about identity with a singular wit and accessibility that makes *Read This
to Get Smarter* an essential guide for curious people of any age. The twenty-first century
offers us countless opportunities to look foolish—in very avoidable ways, in front of lots
of people—but thankfully, Blair is here to help."
– JAMAL JORDAN, AUTHOR OF *QUEER LOVE IN COLOR*

"If you want a deeper understanding of the multi-layer universe of people with disabilities, this
book is a great place to start.
– JILLIAN MERCADO, MODEL, ACTOR, AND FOUNDER OF BLACK DISABLED CREATIVES

"Blair Imani's *Read This to Get Smarter* is a necessary guide for anyone committed to justice
in their personal and political lives. Imani approaches readers with a deep kindness and
offers them concrete tools for thinking anew about race, gender, class, and sexuality, and
for imagining a different kind of world."
– JENNIFER C. NASH, AUTHOR OF *BLACK FEMINISM REIMAGINED*

"I did indeed read this to get smarter, and Blair Imani does not disappoint. As a queer Jew,
to see such thoughtful passages reflecting my own identity left me even more inspired to
continue to educate myself on the history and experiences of others."
– JAKE COHEN, *NEW YORK TIMES* BESTSELLING AUTHOR OF *JEW-ISH: A COOKBOOK*

"I love Blair's style of educating. Her fun and colorful personality (and fashion) really makes
learning fun, but my favorite thing about Blair is how she calls on people affected by a certain
issue or subject to speak on it and amplifies their voices. I wish more educators did that."
– NATHALIE EMMANUEL, ACTOR

READ THIS TO GET SMARTER

READ THIS TO GET SMARTER

ABOUT RACE, CLASS, GENDER, DISABILITY & MORE

BLAIR IMANI

TEN SPEED PRESS
California | New York

Library of Congress Control Number: 2021940688

Trade Paperback ISBN: 978-1-9848-6054-5
eBook ISBN: 978-1-9848-6055-2

Printed in the USA

Editor: Kaitlin Ketchum | Production editor: Kimmy Tejasindhu
Editorial assistant: Want Chyi
Designer: Lauren Rosenberg
Typefaces: Typemate's Cera PRO by Jakob Runge and Adobe Font's Chaparral Pro by Carol Twombly
Production manager: Dan Myers
Copyeditor: Carolyn Keating | Proofreader: Jennifer McClain
Indexer: Ken Della Penta
Publicist: Felix Cruz | Marketer(s): Daniel Wikey and Monica Stanton

3rd Printing

First Edition

TO EVERYBODY WHO HAS EVER BEEN
MADE TO FEEL LIKE A NOBODY.

CONTENTS

INTRODUCTION

Welcome! Thank you for being here. My name is Blair Imani, and I am an author, educator, and historian. I firmly believe that learning is a blessing, and my life is dedicated to learning and helping others learn. First things first: you are already smart. Intelligence is the ability to learn and apply information, and that is something that we all do every day. Even though we are already smart, we can always get smarter about the world, topics we're not deeply familiar with, and the lived experiences of other people. *Read This to Get Smarter* explores how we can become more informed, compassionate, and intentional as we work to better understand ourselves, others, and the systems around us. Getting smarter is a journey, not a destination, and a great deal of our journey will involve unlearning. Patience, mutual respect, and perseverance are important tools to carry along the way.

It might be frustrating to realize that we will never be done in our learning journeys, but it's also exciting because we can constantly transform our perspectives as more accurate information becomes available. Many of the understandings we have been taught and socialized to believe are based on the assumptions of long dead European colonizers who worked to maintain systems of supremacy and dominance instead of presenting fact, evidence, or truth. If we do not prioritize getting smarter, then we deny ourselves the full complexity of the human experience and instead subsist on inadequate and harmful assumptions. It is not my intention to present solutions to the myriad consequences of these assumptions—instead, I offer a starting place to achieve a shared understanding. Inspired by *Smarter in Seconds,* my viral thirty-second microlearning video series, *Read This to Get Smarter* utilizes my signature concision to make abstract and theoretical concepts more concrete in a well-researched, well-presented, and accessible manner. I do my best to educate others from a place of humility, and I am honored that you have dedicated a fraction of your time in this life to learn from and with me.

Read This to Get Smarter is divided into chapters on identity; relationships; class; disability; race and racism; and sex, gender, and sexual Orientation. Starting with ourselves and working outward, my goal with this book is to provide an important foundation of knowledge ready to be expanded. We will get smarter using information that is strongly supported by the decolonized historical and anthropological record, sociology, and the work of scholars past and present. This book contains valuable tools such as charts on terminology and corresponding explanations, guidance for interpersonal interactions such as how to apologize, and a comprehensive timeline on the invention of race. Every journey toward getting smarter is different, so feel free to read this book in order, skip around, and take notes throughout in as much or as little time as you need. Each chapter concludes with reflection questions to help you apply your new understandings—you can think about them, discuss them with a friend, or journal about them. Our very consciousness means we can *Get Smarter* and collectively experience the blessing of learning every single day. Let's get started.

CHAPTER 1

GET SMARTER ABOUT IDENTITY

Before we begin our journey, let's start with *you*. Who are you? The answers to that all-important question are what make up our identity. Any discussion of identity can get abstract and philosophical very quickly; in this chapter, we will discuss identity as the combination of personal and social identity.

Personal identity is the way a person perceives themselves, while *social identity* is the way others perceive them. Personal identity relates to the things that make you uniquely you, such as your interests, beliefs, gender identity, and sexual orientation. And while identity formation is in many ways connected to socialization, only we can ultimately define our personal identity.

Social identity, because it is dictated by those around us and connects to the concept of social belonging, is often prioritized above personal identity in social situations. While social identity can encompass some (or even many) parts of our personal identity, it doesn't always, because who we understand ourselves to be does not always match the way others understand us. For example, as a bisexual woman I am often incorrectly identified by others as a straight woman. The fact that I am sometimes not believed or understood to be bisexual is not because of a personal failure to be "bisexual enough," but is due to *bi-erasure*, which makes bisexuality both invisible and disbelieved. Bisexuals are bisexual despite how other people might perceive us and regardless of whether we are single or in a relationship. In this aspect of identity, my social identity and personal identity do not always align. Stereotypes, erasure, and oppressive systems mean that many of us are perceived in ways that are fundamentally disconnected from our personal reality. Despite this, our personal identity is still valid even if it is not honored externally in our social identity.

One way to understand identity is as a flower with many petals. Picture a favorite flower and imagine that the components that comprise "you"— whether they are personal or social identities—are the petals on that flower. I picture myself as a sunflower with many petals that represent my gender identity as a woman, my sexual orientation as bisexual, my religious identity as Muslim, my racialized identity as Black, my national identity as American, the languages I speak as English and Spanish, my relationships, my career fields, and my interests. These petals can shed, grow, and change as we go through life, and we are allowed to have as many or as few as we decide. With this understanding we can be reassured that few people look at a flower and judge it by how many petals it has. Rather, we accept a flower as a beautiful and unique whole. Whether you're as complex as an orchid or as minimalistic as a tulip, you're a radiant part of the garden of life. Before I started thinking of identity in this way, I considered the petals of who I am to be too numerous and cumbersome. When I listed the parts of my identity, I thought I had to trim them down a bit—for example, when I converted to Islam in 2015, I felt that I had to remove one identity label in order to make room for my new religious identity. Society made me feel like my identity was too much, too *other*, and too different—but that is not true at all. Who we are is real and valid regardless of whether we are understood by others.

NAMES

As you already know, my name is Blair Imani. You might not know, however, that my parents named me Blair Elizabeth. The name that we are given at birth is usually called our "birth name" or "given name." In some communities, the name that appears on government documents is called a "government name." Whether you call this name your birth name, government name, or given name, it may be different from what you go by in the world. And that's okay. Names are often the first or only thing that people know about us. So it makes sense that we should like and feel comfortable with our names. And if we don't, we can change them. That's what I did! At various times in my life I did not like my birth name. I've always liked the name "Blair," but I never much cared for "Elizabeth." When I was a child, this was because Elizabeth was difficult for me to spell. Once I mastered the spelling, I still didn't like the name though, because to me it was a white woman's name. And while ideally names should not be racialized, the fact that they often are is a reality. As time went on, I started to realize that when people read the name "Blair Elizabeth," they didn't picture *me*. The most poignant instance of this was when I was hired for a position at a law firm. I was surprised because they hired me right over the phone. They saw my resume, read my name, and felt that I would be a perfect fit.

When I arrived for my first day, on time and ready to go, I sat in the lobby for about thirty minutes. Any time I attempted to make my presence known, I was assured that I would be helped in due time. An adept eavesdropper, I eventually overheard the receptionist asking herself, "Where is this Blair girl?" I politely cleared my throat and said "Hello!" Again, I was assured that she would be right with me. The receptionist finally decided to call the new hire, Blair, to see if she was coming in. My phone rang. I answered the phone while making direct eye contact with the shocked receptionist. The firm had hired someone far more "diverse" than anticipated. Blair Elizabeth was not, as they had assumed, a white woman, but a Black woman. In fact, I learned then and there that I was the first Black person to be hired in the company's decades-long history. *Oops!*

As part of our personal and social identities, names help to distinguish us from the rest of the world. They can be formally given to us as young people by our caretakers, be given to us as nicknames by other family members or friends, and/or be chosen by ourselves. At the most basic level, names are just collections of letters and their associated sounds. Of course, in practice it is rarely that simple. Which names and how many we have—as well as their spellings, pronunciations, and cultural associations—usually constitutes part of our social identity. Beyond that, which names are legally allowed or banned is often defined by institutions such as governments. In the United States, laws for names may differ slightly from state to state. Character limits are imposed so that names can be recorded in state databases, and obscenity laws dictate which names are not allowed. Numbers and symbols in names may be allowed in some states and banned in others, while some allow numbers and symbols but require that they be spelled out. (For example, I could name my child Asterisk, but on their birth certificate, I could not write it simply as "*.") Outside of legal parameters there are also social parameters for "acceptable names." What is and is not "acceptable" for names has to do with social norms and biases that connect to race, gender, and more.

Have you ever met someone named Thomas who goes by "Tom"? Or someone who goes by their middle name, or another name that's not part of their legal name or birth name? We call these nicknames, and they are a great example of how we are generally expected to use—and are comfortable using—the names a person decides to go by, even if they differ from their legal or birth names. In turn, we expect people to use the names we choose to be called, and consider the remembering and proper usage of names an important act of respect.

In my case, I felt that my birth name carried a connotation that did not resonate with me, so I changed it from "Blair Elizabeth" to "Blair Imani." *Imani* is a Kiswahili word meaning "faith," which was perfect for me because I changed my name during the same time period that I converted to Islam. I also like that it's five letters, just like my first name, and think it sounds good, which is important to me. My mom was initially not super enthusiastic about my using a name that she didn't pick, which was awkward. But she has since accepted it. My dad was pretty cool with it, as many of his friends changed their names during the 1960s and '70s to ones they felt better represented their African heritage. Most importantly, I love my name. Whether others approve or disapprove of my name change—or anyone else's name change—does not matter. People will continue to practice self-definition and self-naming for various reasons. I am comfortable sharing the reasons why I changed my name, but others might not be. While we may be curious as to why people go by one name or another, we don't actually need to know the reasoning for a name alteration or change in order to respect and use it correctly.

PRONUNCIATION

Learning to correctly pronounce other people's names to the best of our individual abilities is an important part of respecting their identity. Having your name butchered every time you meet a new person can be exhausting and invalidating. My partner, Akeem, used to go by the name "Keem," a childhood nickname that was often easier for others to pronounce. Akeem still regularly has to answer the question "Is it *ha*-keem, *uh*-keem, or *ah*-keem?" (it's *uh*-keem), but as an adult it's much easier to manage. Akeem doesn't mind answering the question "How do I pronounce your name?"

to people who ask respectfully. It's dismissive, hurtful, and unnecessary to comment on someone's name or tell them that it's too difficult. Making the effort to learn how to pronounce other people's names properly is a great way to show that we respect and care about them.

One way to get smarter about name pronunciation is to remember that there is no such thing as "difficult names" or "easy names." There are simply names you are familiar with and names you have yet to come across—and there are certainly more of the latter than the former. When I meet someone with a name I haven't encountered before, I take the time to learn it. If I'm communicating with someone verbally, I'll ask them to repeat their name if I didn't catch it the first time. I want to make sure I'm not butchering their name and disrespecting them in the process. I am often able to emulate the sounds other people make to me, but not everyone can hear or speak. If you have a hearing or speaking disability, pronouncing someone's name as they tell it to you might be something that you struggle with or cannot do. And that's okay (we'll examine ableism and disability in chapter 4). Sometimes I learn better if something is written down, so I may ask the person to spell out their name. We all learn differently and should determine what works best for each of us. I've often found that people who have unique names will be ready with a quick way to learn it by rhyming it with a more familiar word. If someone ever notes that you've pronounced their name incorrectly, thank them for letting you know, ask them to repeat their name aloud, and move on. As stated by actress Uzo Aduba's mother, "If they can learn to pronounce Tchaikovsky and Michaelangelo and Dostoyevsky, they can learn Uzoamaka."

GENDER

Many names have gendered meanings or connotations, which can differ within and across communities and contexts. My first name, Blair, is understood by many as being gender neutral, which was part of the reason my parents chose it for me. Feminine, masculine, or gender-neutral names may shape or express other elements of our personal identity, like gender identity and gender expression. (We'll talk more about gender in chapter 6.) Gender associations for names differ greatly across cultures and communities—for example, in the United States the name "Sasha" may be perceived as feminine, while in Russia it may be considered masculine.

If a person doesn't identify with the gender associated with their name, they may change it to a name that better affirms their gender. For my friend Milo, choosing a name that better aligned with his gender identity was an important part of his transition. As people in his life began and continued to use his correct name, he felt affirmed and respected by them. Conversely, as people struggled to learn and implement his name, he felt disrespected, even though he knew in some cases that it was a genuine mistake. And while it's natural to make mistakes, especially when learning something new, intention and impact are not the same thing, and mistakes can still be hurtful. Whether or not someone *intends* to disrespect us doesn't change the feeling of being disrespected.

DEAD NAMES

When a person changes their name as part of the process of gender affirmation, their previous name is often called their "former name" or their "dead name," and it's generally harmful to use or ask about someone's dead name. My former name, Blair Elizabeth, would not be considered my dead name because I am cisgender and did not change it as part of gender affirmation or transition. The pervasiveness of transphobia and a general lack of education about the diversity of gender has resulted in many people refusing to use a transgender or nonbinary person's correct name, which is called *deadnaming*. Deadnamers might have no problem calling their cisgender friend "Harry" instead of "Harold," but with the added layer of transphobia, they may claim that it's completely unreasonable for them to use a transgender, nonbinary, or gender-nonconforming person's correct and current name. This is not only wrong but is incredibly disrespectful and harmful to a person's sense of self. Deadnamers may also press people to share their "real names" (by which they mean their dead names), but someone's real name is the name they currently use.

All you need to know about someone's name is what they share with you. The way to avoid deadnaming and being disrespectful is to get smarter about transphobia, which we'll do in chapter 6, and always use—and not question—a person's name as they tell it to you. End of story. This goes for people you've never met as well as people you already know who may have changed their name or are currently going by a different name. If someone tells you they are using a different name than they did previously, make your best effort to remember and always use their current name. If you make a mistake and use their former name or dead name, it is usually best to briefly apologize and move on. Understand that saying "I'm sorry" doesn't always mean that an apology will be or must be immediately accepted, especially when the same mistake or harm is repeated. Pairing an apology with a statement of intention is an excellent way to demonstrate respect and trustworthiness. Instead of saying, "I'm sorry," you could say, for example, "I'm sorry, I know your name is Lucy. I will work on getting it right, because I want you to know that I respect you." Try not to "overapologize." Overapologizing happens when our heightened concern around offending or hurting someone ends up being harmful itself. Avoid making the situation about how badly *you* feel. Doing that is called "centering your feelings," and it can distract from the person you may have offended or disrespected. (See page 53 for more on how to apologize.)

Keep in mind that a person may give permission to use their former or dead name when referencing them from before they changed their name, but this depends on the individual. For example, if you had a childhood friend that you knew by one name but who is now known as "Diana," they might feel respected if you refer to them as Diana even when you are referencing them in the past when they did not yet go by that name. Or, Diana might be okay with you using the name they used as a child when referencing them in the past. Everyone is different. When in doubt, and depending on your relationship with that person, it is best to respectfully ask them what to do, but take care to avoid coming from a place of entitlement when asking about the details of a person's life, such as names they may have used previously.

NAMES AND BIAS

Whether or not a name is "common" often depends on what you consider "common" to be, which is extremely subjective. In the United States, *Mary, John, Michael,* and *Joseph* have been among the most popular names for decades. This is due to the influence of Christianity, since all these names appear in the Bible. In Spanish-speaking countries, the names *Maria, Juan, Miguel,* and *José* are equally common for the same reason. The name *Jesus* (pronounced hey-*ZOOZ*) is also extremely popular in Spanish-speaking countries, but *Jesus* (pronounced *GEE*-zuhs) is not as popular in English-speaking ones.

During classroom roll calls, it's common for teachers to ask students what name they would like to be called in class. (Ideally, this happens over email prior to roll calls so there's no embarrassing moment when a name someone doesn't use is read aloud and might embarrass the student in question.) This happened often when I was in elementary school; my Taiwanese friends would have their Mandarin names on school documents and go by their self-described American names in class. This is pretty common, though the reasons for this practice differs by person. In some cases, it might be to help the student connect to and form a sense of belonging to a dominant culture, and in other cases it might be to avoid teachers and classmates mispronouncing a name, or to avoid xenophobic or racist bias. Of course, going by another name isn't a guaranteed way to escape bias, but individuals are entitled to make their own choices—and even change their minds—about their names. We may never know why someone goes by a particular name, and we're not entitled to know.

The biases and assumptions applied to different names have consequences, especially when those names indicate that a person is outside the dominant culture. One study on the subject consistently found that on resumes, names that seem to belong to a white person are more likely to receive a response than names that are perceived to belong to a Black or Asian person. In addition to changing their names to something that sounds like it belongs to a white person, job applicants often remove any indicators of their race from their resumes, including club memberships or work at organizations that primarily serve racialized people. These "whitened resumes" consistently receive more callbacks than those that better reflect an individual's cultural or racialized context. My father, DeWalt, often put the name *Walter* on his resume and applications in order to avoid the anti-Black racial biases that came with his name, and he confirmed anecdotally that resumes where he used the name *Walter* received more callbacks than resumes where he used *DeWalt*, despite the resumes being otherwise identical. The problem with name-based biases is not the names themselves, but the racist, classist, and xenophobic systems that prevent people with non-Eurocentric names from being treated, understood, and hired equitably. Names are just the collections of letters and sounds that we call ourselves, and no one should feel entitled to make judgments about or be prejudiced toward a person based on them.

LAST NAMES

When I was a child, my father jokingly told me that he did not have a middle name because his family could not afford one, so I spent a significant part of my childhood believing that you had to pay for additional names. When I asked why my brother's middle name was the same as my father's first name, he told me it was so he didn't have to buy a new one. (Reader, this is a classic dad joke, not based in any historical fact.) In reality, middle names are common in some cultures and not in others. The same is true of last names. In Indonesia, it is common for everyday people to have only a single name, or mononym. And in the United States, while there are people who are popularly known by mononyms like Cher or Common, it is legally required that every citizen have a first and last name.

There is great diversity in the ways that we end up with our last names. My last name came from my father. A name taken from one's father is called *patronymic*, and in the United States patronymic last names are extremely common. Prior to the 1970s, patronymic names were mandatory in some states, but this changed after many legal challenges were made to this archaic and blatantly patriarchal law. Families are extremely diverse, and not everyone has a father as part of their family, so it is important to remember that this is not the best or only way for last names to be passed down. Everyone in my immediate family has the same last name. As such, ours might be called our "family name" because it is the name we all share. It is also common for people to have different last names than their family members, whether that is due to adoption, marriage, personal decisions, or other individual circumstances. Getting smarter about last names means recognizing that families come in different forms, have different arrangements and traditions, and make different decisions (which we will learn more about in chapter 2).

Eurocentric approaches to history often claim that people in eleventh-century England were the first to use last names, but names relating to families and clans were used in cultures such as ancient Japan since at least 300 CE. A last name can indicate an individual's family history or ancestry, community of origin, region of origin, religious background, and ethnic group or tribal membership. Names such as *Smith*, *Cooper*, and *Fisher* are last names associated with the professions of blacksmithing, barrel making, and fishing, respectively, and generally connect in some way to a European ancestry. Names associated with occupations are not exclusive to the English language, however—the Italian last name *Pescatore* and the Dutch last name *Visser* both mean "fisher" and relate to the profession of fishing. In Iceland and other Scandinavian cultures, a last name may reflect a patronymic naming convention. If a father is named Jón, then his son may have the last name Jónsson, while his daughter will have the last name Jónsdóttir, and his nonbinary child the last name Jónsbur. The inclusion of *-bur* as a nonbinary last name suffix began in 2019, and means "child of" instead of "son of" (*-son*) or "daughter of" (*-dóttir*).

The naming conventions of Europe are not the only or best ones, despite Eurocentric assertions. The Yorùbá people, for example, who comprise an ethnic majority in Nigeria, have unique naming practices. Nigerian linguist and educator Kọ́lá Túbọ̀sún has researched and meticulously recorded Yorùbá last names as well as names from other ethnic groups in Nigeria, including the Igbo and Hausa peoples. Túbọ̀sún's own full last name (Ọlátúbọ̀sún) means "success continues to expand." There are many common last names among Yorùbá peoples, like *Adebayo*, *Ojo*, and *Ogunade*, which can also be written using tone marks as *Adébáyò*, *Òjó*, and *Ògúnadé*. Individuals with these last names may have a shared ancestry across the African diaspora, but not always.

In the United States, the last names of many Black Americans are connected to the forced labor of our enslaved ancestors during chattel slavery. Enslaved people rarely had any agency to name themselves. My ancestor Cato Bobo had no choice in his last name, which came from his enslavers at the Bobo Plantation and was forced upon all the people they enslaved. Cato Bobo's name reflected the hideous fact that he was owned and treated as property. His mother likely was not even able to choose his first name without the "permission" of the people who owned her. Today many Black Americans have traditionally "European sounding" last names because our ancestors suffered the inhumanity of slavery under people with those last names. In some context these names are referenced as "slave names," but this term is often used pejoratively and should be avoided in most contexts. At the end of the Civil War, the last names Freedman, Freedmen, and Freeman became popular among newly freed people, because this represented a rejection of an enslaved past and a future where freedom was a defining feature. Many people like Cato Bobo did not change their last names when they were freed. This was not because they were comfortable with the connection between their last names and their enslavement, but because for many descendants of enslaved people, these names were a way to trace their lineages, reconnect, and be found by their family after emancipation through registries called slave schedules. After Reconstruction, it continued to be commonplace for Black Americans to change their last names and create or choose new ones connecting to their African heritage. One prominent example of this is the early traditions of the Nation of Islam that encouraged believers to reject their "slave names" and replace their last names with an X, which signified the fact that enslavement had prevented them from knowing their true family names. Pan Africanist human rights activist El Hajj Malik El Shabazz, who is still known popularly as Malcolm X, is one prominent Black American who practiced this.

Like all names, last names are essentially made up. Empowered by this, many families choose to break with patronymic and patriarchal naming traditions to create a portmanteau of their last names, or to choose a new name to create a shared identifier that represents their shared life. Two friends of mine with the last names *Scott* and *Stevens* combined them to create a completely new last name reflective of the journey that they would embark on together as the *Scovens* family. The tradition of taking on the last name of one's partner isn't something everyone participates in, which we'll discuss more in chapter 2. Some people may replace their original last name with their partner's last name, some may take their partner's last name and retain their original last name as a middle name, and some may keep their own name, sometimes adding a hyphen. At the end of the day, there is no right or wrong way to name yourself and respecting other people's names is always necessary.

PRONOUNS

She, *he*, and *they* are third-person pronouns and are used to refer to someone without using their name. The pronouns we use are part of our personal identity and are sometimes connected to our gender identity. (Note that not all languages use pronouns, so this section will be focused on English.) Just as we cannot reasonably assume a person's name before we have learned it, we likewise cannot know someone's pronouns just by looking at them or knowing their name. We have been socialized to believe that we *can* know things about someone's personal identity by looking at them, but that isn't the case. Getting pronouns correct—that is, not assuming whether a person uses *he*, *she*, *they*, another pronoun, or no pronouns at all—is important. Honoring and using a person's correct pronouns demonstrates respect and acknowledgment of the person and their identity. This is similar to learning to properly pronounce someone's name as a way to show them respect and care. Conversely, disrespecting a person's correct pronouns is harmful and can have serious consequences related to mental health outcomes. Pronouns are not obvious, and part of getting smarter means relearning how we think about them.

When I was growing up, it was common to see the pronoun "he" used as a default to reference nonspecific people (a vestige of patriarchy baked into language). For example, you might see "Parents, your child is important to us. We will see that he gets the best education from our school." While the school in this example may have been co-ed, "he" was simply used as a default pronoun. Moving toward inclusion, references of "he or she" or "s/he" became more commonplace, though they still reflect a gender binary. Today, "they" is often used as a singular third-person pronoun when the pronouns of a person are not known. In English, we do this quite naturally all the time. For example, if you are at a gathering and there's an unclaimed jacket on the couch afterward, you might inform the host by saying, "Someone left their jacket" rather than "Someone left his or her jacket." It has become increasingly common for people, for a variety of reasons, to use "they/them" as their personal pronouns rather than using gendered pronouns. Unfortunately, people who object to using or respecting the use of they/them pronouns often point to "grammar" as the reason they cannot use someone's correct pronoun. These people are both disrespectful and incorrect: the singular "they" in the English language dates back to the 1300s. Regardless, grammar is a pathetic excuse to deny someone their humanity and not use their correct pronouns. Getting smarter about pronouns means understanding why we are so committed to using certain pronouns for certain people based on our own assumptions, when pronouns are ultimately a personal matter that should easily be reflected by society.

For many people, pronouns and gender are connected, but that's not the case for everyone. The ways in which gender identity and pronouns overlap—or don't—are personal to individuals, so we shouldn't assume a universal approach. Many English-speaking people, whether they are cisgender or transgender, do use the traditional binary pronouns as representations of their gender identity—for example, a woman who uses she/her pronouns. But just because someone uses she/her pronouns does not necessarily or automatically mean that her gender identity is "woman." Likewise, if someone uses they/them pronouns, that does not mean they are nonbinary. Some people are comfortable with both she/her or he/him and they/them. Some people use *neopronouns*, which are newer to language, including but not limited to *xe*, *zir*, *em*, and *thon*. While this may seem confusing or "nonstandard English," it's important to remember that every word that we use with confidence and regularity was once new to the language and completely unknown to us. We constantly learn new words, and that will include new pronouns.

When you meet a new person, it's polite to give them your pronouns as well as your name, which may encourage the other person to do the same. (This is assuming that both you and the other person use pronouns—some people don't use them at all, which is also valid.) I might say, "Hi! I'm Blair, and my pronouns are she/her. It's lovely to meet you!" If someone doesn't offer their pronouns or you're unaware of a person's correct pronouns, it is generally appropriate to use "they/them" pronouns to avoid misgendering the person. It's also generally okay to inquire about someone's pronouns if you do so respectfully and neutrally—for example, "May I ask your pronouns?" Some discussions of pronouns use the term *preferred pronouns,* but this is now generally discouraged. As noted by Jeffrey Marsh, gender theorist and author of *How to Be You,* discussing pronouns as a matter of "preference" is part of a harmful legacy of characterizing anything outside of strict heteronormative and cisnormative definitions as "lifestyles" or "preferences." When personal identity is discussed in terms of "preference," it often results in the perception that respecting a person's identity is optional instead of mandatory. The exception to this guidance would be individuals who use more than one set of pronouns—for example, those who use or are comfortable with "she/her" *and* "they/them" pronouns—and may prefer one set above the other. In such a case, discussing preferred pronouns is fine, but in general, it's best to ask someone which pronouns they "use" or what their pronouns "are" versus asking what pronouns they "prefer." If someone does not use pronouns, then you can just use that person's name or follow that person's specific guidance (note how in this sentence I have used "that person's" rather than the pronoun "their"—easy!).

Sometimes when we speak to people, we do so on autopilot, relying on assumptions instead of information and moving quickly instead of being present and thinking before we interact. Pronoun usage reflects the importance of intentional communication with the people in our lives. When we have a conversation with someone, we are sharing part of our life with them, however brief. Get smarter about pronouns by remembering that we have been incorrectly taught that *our perceptions* of people are more important than *their reality*, and that must change. Pronouns are personal, and when we misspeak or fail to use someone's correct pronouns, it is more than an error—it's invalidating a person's experience and reality. When we refer to others, we should do so on their terms. Not on ours.

Do your best to make a habit of offering, asking for, and properly using the pronouns of everyone you meet, just like we do with our names. If you are still becoming accustomed to the pronouns a person uses and fail to get it right, refer back to our discussion about deadnaming (page 9) and see the section on apologizing (page 53), as similar guidance applies here. Doing better in the future is extremely important.

VALUES AND BELIEFS

When I was growing up, my parents would often tell me they weren't there to tell me *what* to think, but rather to show me *how* to think. However, a lot of what I learned in terms of my beliefs and values did come from my parents, particularly my inclination toward advocacy and the pursuit of knowledge. An important part of learning how to think is doing something called *critical thinking*, which is a crucial life skill. With a solid understanding of critical thinking, we are able to examine and reevaluate our values and beliefs. Everything that we have come to understand, believe, and value connects deeply to our sense of self. As a result, when our understandings, beliefs, and values are challenged by new information (even if that information is rooted firmly in fact and evidence), we may become defensive or reject the new information. But it's important to tap into critical thinking and keep an open mind even when presented with information we may find challenging. Critical thinking can help us fight something called *confirmation bias*, which is the propensity to seek out information that aligns with what we already believe and value, even if that information is poorly sourced, skewed, and biased. Because of confirmation bias, it's important that we actively interrogate our own beliefs and seek out credible sources of information to help inform us—otherwise, we can get into a cycle of only engaging with information we agree with, which doesn't allow us to learn and grow. When seeking out information, try to use trustworthy sources and materials. This means examining the research that has gone into the materials (which you can do in this book's Bibliography section), determining the qualifications of the individuals who are providing the information (which you can find in the About the Author section of this book), and understanding how the materials came to be funded and published and by whom (which you can do on the copyright page of this book). These are necessary steps to take to avoid becoming misled by false but well-presented information.

Values are our personal road maps for evaluating what is good and righteous as well as what is bad and harmful. Contrary to what we learn as young people, the world cannot be easily split into a binary of good and evil. There's a lot of nuance and gray areas in between. For example, if we conflate the word *legal* with "good," we might end up supporting policies that are dehumanizing and violent just because an institution says they're okay. However, if we can critically examine our values, we can bridge the disconnects and come to an understanding that is in line with our values. Values shape how we treat ourselves and others. For example, the mythology of the United States says that as a country we value "liberty and justice for all." In practice, however, this value often falls short of implementation. The United States has the largest population of incarcerated people in the world—what is liberty for people in chains? Critical thinking allows us to be honest with ourselves and examine the reality that the United States is not living up to its values.

Beliefs are what we hold to be true about ourselves, others, and the world at large. For example, maybe you believe that all human beings should be treated with dignity and respect. I certainly do. Maybe you admire the phrase from the US Constitution that states that "all men are created equal." While that phrase seems fine, yet sexist, when taken at face value, it takes on a different meaning when you consider the fact that the man who wrote it was Thomas Jefferson, who enslaved more than 600 people in his lifetime. The fact that Jefferson was an enslaver makes it abundantly clear that he believed in white supremacy. There is a massive disconnect therefore between the belief that "all men are created equal" and the incorrect belief that "white men are predestined to own and dominate all other human beings." Beliefs about how power should and should not be distributed are political beliefs, and political beliefs can be deeply divisive because they concern everything from how money and resources are controlled to how human rights are protected (or not), and so much more. While it's okay for people to have differing political beliefs, if an individual's beliefs are dehumanizing, you are allowed to reject those beliefs. You do not have to "see the other side" of an argument if the other side is rooted in denying other people's humanity and dignity and disrespecting others. As long as a person's beliefs do not promote harming and oppressing others, they are an important way of forming understanding and meaning.

Beliefs do not have to be based in logic, fact, or evidence to be important and valid. The aspects of human understanding that are not based in concrete, material, or physical things are sometimes described as faith, or spiritual and religious beliefs. Religion is defined differently in different contexts, so instead of using a definition that may inadvertently be exclusive, we'll keep in mind that religions may or may not have elements related to a belief in a higher power, like a god (monotheism), multiple gods (polytheism), or no god(s) (nontheism). Sometimes religious beliefs are formalized through doctrine or scripture. Religions can be ancient or relatively recent. Religious beliefs often—but don't always—include rituals, prayers, ways of living and dressing, dietary restrictions, and days of celebration. When we talk about spirituality and religion, it is important not to rely on assumptions. It may be easy to assume other people have the same beliefs you do, particularly if you're not familiar with other belief systems. If you grew up in a predominantly Christian community, you might automatically assume that everyone celebrates Christmas. But of course not everyone does. Since so many companies and businesses in the United States close on Christian holidays, one way to include people with different belief systems is to add a "floating" holiday that workers can use to observe religious holidays for which the business does not usually close. This is becoming increasingly common, and is a good way to be inclusive of all religions and belief systems.

For some people (like me), faith and/or religion are at the core of their personal and/or social identity. For others (like my best friend, Ren), this couldn't be further from the truth, which is perfectly okay. It is also the case that some people may view the same ritual or practice in different contexts. Something like a shower in the morning might just be a hygienic practice for one person, but for another it might be a spiritual practice or cleansing ritual as well. It is important not to rely on biased understandings or assumptions about religion and people of faith. Being religious does not mean that an individual is conservative or anti-science—they *might* be conservative and anti-science, but that should not be assumed one way or the other based only on their religion. Furthermore, we cannot rely on the visual or cultural indicators we have been taught to believe are associated with different religious practices and apply them to people without knowing more about who they are. Just like we shouldn't assume that all *Star Trek* fans speak Klingon, it's inappropriate to assume that all Jewish people speak Hebrew or that all Muslims speak Arabic.

I converted to Islam in 2015, and first experienced the assumptions that go along with religion when I began working in an office. During the holy month of Ramadan, it is common for Muslims to participate in a physical fast from food and water during daylight hours and to also fast from materialism, distractions, and harmful actions. This period is one of sacred reflection where meditation and mindfulness are crucial, and emphasis is placed on compassion to humanity in the form of zakat, or charity. Assumptions about Muslims and Islam have led to the misconception that all Muslims participate in Ramadan in the same manner, which is not true. Due to the medications I take, I cannot fast from food and water, and many other people might not fast for medical and other personal reasons, or because they are pregnant, disabled, menstruating, or traveling. My non-Muslim coworkers were perplexed when they saw me still eating lunch during Ramadan, because they incorrectly assumed that there was only one way to be Muslim and only one way to participate in Ramadan. As an educator, I was happy to teach my coworkers about Islam, but it's important not to expect members of religious communities to take on the labor of educating you about their religion—especially when there are search engines and supercomputers at our fingertips. Getting smarter about religion means understanding that our beliefs may differ from those around us, including people within our own religious community (if we have one).

REFLECTION QUESTIONS

- What does your name mean? Where does it come from?
- Do you consider some names to be more "legitimate" than others? Do certain names or spellings seem "better" or "lesser" to you? Why, and if so, what steps can you take to fight that bias?
- Have you thought to yourself (or even said out loud) that someone's name was too difficult to learn? Why?
- Do you use pronouns? What are your pronouns, and why do you use them?

- How can you help to normalize sharing and asking for personal pronouns in your life? For example, you might ask if your company or school will consider adding pronouns to business cards or email signatures. This is a great step to take as long as the policy includes people that do not use personal pronouns.

- What are some of your core values and beliefs? Which were passed down to you from your family, and which have you picked up from your friends and your community? Which did you develop through experience?

- What are some beliefs that you consider to be tied to your identity? Have these changed over time for you? What is something that you currently believe that you previously did not (or vice versa)?

- What incorrect assumptions have other people made about you because of your beliefs? How did it make you feel? Have you ever made incorrect assumptions about other people based on their beliefs?

CHAPTER 2

GET SMARTER ABOUT RELATIONSHIPS

Relationships describe the ways people are connected. In the past century, "relationship" has come to describe romantic or intimate connections between people, but here we are using it to describe any type of connection between ourselves and others. We have many different relationships, and use language to describe how we are connected (or not connected) to others. Since the fourteenth century the English word *stranger* has been used to describe people we don't know or aren't familiar with. Given that there are more than seven billion people on Earth, most of us are strangers to each other. For those we are closer to, we use words such as *friend*, *family*, *kin*, *partner*, or *loved one* to describe these deeper connections. Whether we are connected directly, indirectly, or not at all, the one unifying factor we share is that we are all part of humanity.

The ancient Bantu philosophy of *ubuntu*, translated as "humanity toward others" or "I am because you are," informs my approach to all my relationships. Also understood as "mutual respect," ubuntu requires us to acknowledge the humanity of the other parties in every relationship and in every interaction as a matter of principle. Acknowledging and honoring the humanity of everyone we interact with is one of the most basic elements of sharing our lives with others. In addition to "humanity toward others," ubuntu focuses on our own interconnected and communal nature: "I am because you are." In a world full of dehumanization from oppressive structures and biases, it can be a significant challenge to honor the humanity of all individuals whether or not we agree with them, like them, or feel remotely connected to them. But ubuntu is necessary for getting smarter about relationships. Beginning all our interactions with a promise of mutual respect and a shared understanding of our shared humanity can fundamentally disrupt many of the harmful things we have been taught to believe about ourselves and others.

All relationships, even the ones we are born into, should start from a place of honoring our humanity and understanding our interconnectedness. Ubuntu is a humbling philosophy because it calls on us to understand that our actions impact more people than just ourselves, and that our interconnectedness requires us to respect the humanity of everyone, not just those we have been socialized to believe are deserving.

Sometimes we are expected to "earn respect" or behave a certain way to be perceived as "respectable," but respect and humanity should be inherent to all. This doesn't mean we have to become best friends with everyone we come across, or that we should overlook a harm someone has done, but it does mean we must acknowledge the humanity of all people, even those we dislike. While respect should not have to be earned, trust certainly should. Trust is the belief and confidence that we have in others—and that others have in us—and it plays a role in all relationships to some degree. In long-term relationships, trust is based on the demonstrated promises of care, reliability, and security. Being part of a community requires us to put our trust in each other. Depending on the type of relationship, trust may be earned through the fulfillment of responsibilities and expectations. For example, elected officials have a responsibility to their constituents, and this is traditionally codified through legislation or policies—whether constituents trust elected officials has a lot to do with whether those officials or the institutions they represent support and enact policies that their constituents value. In other circumstances where relationships are less formally defined, expectations and the fulfillment of them can be created and reinforced through cultural and social norms. Accordingly, the way that we determine what is and is not trustworthy behavior can be dictated by cultural and social norms. Privacy, which can be deeply connected to trust, is something that operates very differently across generations and cultures. In my family, it is expected that if somebody tells you something that is very personal to them, you do not share it with others without that person's consent, but this is not always the case for everyone. Because of my familial context, if someone shares information that I have shared with them without my consent, I may treat it as a violation of my trust and privacy regardless of whether I explicitly stated they should keep that information private. Part of getting smarter about trust means learning how to communicate our expectations. Yet even when we do this, we may not always have those expectations met, because not everyone is trustworthy. It may also take time to determine whether someone is trustworthy by observing their behavior, actions, and words. Trusting other people, especially those we do not know well, can put us in a very vulnerable position, and when we violate other people's trust, it can be difficult to rebuild. Building trust is further complicated by various external and internal factors, such as systems of oppression, institutions, social expectations, personal boundaries, and our own previous experiences. In this chapter, we will focus on getting smarter about family, friendship, and intimate partnerships, as well as on how to maintain healthy relationships.

FAMILY

In the United States, *family* is generally defined as a group of two or more people who are related by birth, marriage, or adoption and reside together. This limited and technical definition of family is used to quickly and easily categorize people in order to track households for the census and other government programs. Other institutions, like religious organizations, may also enforce definitions of family that are not in alignment with human diversity and lived experience. In media such as movies, books, and TV shows, family is often depicted as a "nuclear" family consisting of a mother, father, and two children, which became popularized in the mid-twentieth century when American propaganda used it to reinforce notions of the American Dream (and who had access to it). These depictions of family were usually—and often still are—primarily white, heterosexual, middle-class, and abled. Just because these types of families have historically been the only ones represented does not mean that other kinds of families have not always existed. As long as there have been people, there has been an incredible amount of diversity in our individual identities and how we have formed our families. Getting smarter about families is crucial to expanding our understanding of ourselves and others.

FAMILY STRUCTURES

Part of getting smarter about family means being aware of the incredible diversity of family structures, and not making assumptions about them. Growing up, my older brother and sister would often go to their mother's house on the weekends. As a result, I thought that everyone's older siblings went to their mother's house on the weekend. It was not until I was about eight years old that one of my friends asked me why my brother was never home on the weekends, and that was the first time I realized that not every family is structured like mine. That was also when I learned the term *half-brother*. My older siblings and I have the same father, but we have different mothers. Our family is referred to as a "blended" family, where one or both parents have children from a previous relationship. It was so blended that I thought all families were like mine, which was the intention of my parents and my father's co-parents. *Coparenting* is when individuals who are not romantic partners share the responsibilities of raising a child. As a young adult, I noticed that people would preface explanations of their family structure with "my family is a little different" before diving into what that difference meant, but I never heard someone say "my family is pretty standard." This is because difference is part of what it means to be human, and there's no such thing as "the norm," even if it's defined that way by the government or other institutions. And because differences are so common, narrowly fitting into the norm is often the more rare occurrence. Even if your family structure is not statistically common, if it works for you and your family members, that is enough. Understanding how diverse families can be—and not making assumptions about other people's family arrangements—makes us more conscientious members of the human family.

One of the ways we can be smarter, kinder, and more respectful to others is to use language that reflects the diverse nature of family structures. It's limiting to assume that everyone has a mom, or a mom and a dad, or married parents—and these assumptions can be disrespectful. For example, rather than referring to a child's "parents" or their "mom and dad," calling the child's guardian(s) their "adult(s)" or "grown-up(s)" is a concise and simple way to avoid inadvertently contributing to the stigma and erasure of single parents, same-gender parents, foster parents, or nonparent guardians like older siblings, grandparents, or more communal families. Along the same lines, when it comes to Mother's Day and Father's Day, many schools and classrooms are starting to shift to celebrating Guardian Appreciation Day, a nongendered day of gratitude and appreciation for caretakers. In addition to working to expand our own understanding of family, it's important that we do that same work to change institutions like schools to reflect the many types of families that exist.

It is also important not to impose our assumptions or prejudices on someone's family structure. For my friends with older parents, it was sometimes assumed that they were being raised by their grandparents; and while many people are raised by their grandparents or in multi-generational family structures, it is our responsibility to work through our assumptions and biases about age and raising children, not the responsibility of others to debunk them. People decide to have children—or not—at different ages and shouldn't be forced to deal with other people's prejudices simply because their decisions exist outside of the parameters of social expectations. When or if a family or individual chooses to have children, their choice is valid and should be respected. Furthermore, if someone's parent isn't part of the family structure, it should not be assumed that this is because of death, divorce, absence, or another tragedy. While that may be the case for some of us, making this assumption automatically, particularly when it's related to other forms of bias, like racism, is harmful and disrespectful. Two-parent families are not the best or only type of family, and single-parent families are valid family structures, even as social stigma and bias dictate otherwise. Divorce, death, incarceration, miscarriage, and other common yet stigmatized aspects of family do not mean that a family is unsuccessful or broken. Just because a certain type of family isn't depicted in the media or familiar to us doesn't mean it's not a valid one.

ADOPTION

Adoption, whether through formal or informal processes, has existed throughout human history, but because it is considered outside of the traditional family structure it is often stigmatized or viewed as less important than biological families. Of course, this is untrue—whether you are connected by birth, adoption, or otherwise, all family matters. My mother, Krissy, was born without a name. She was designated as "Baby Girl" until she was adopted by my late grandparents Roy and Eloise. Adoption is one of many ways that families are formed and there are many types of adoption. The people who pass on their genes to us are not always the same people who raise us or whom we call our parents. My mother was adopted as an infant by people she was not biologically related to and she was informed that she was adopted when she was a child, though this does not always happen due to various circumstances. Some people never learn they were adopted or may only learn in adulthood. In other cases, people may be adopted by someone they are related to but who is not their biological parent. Sometimes people are adopted by their stepparents. My grandparents decided to adopt because they could not have children, so they joined the countless people who create their families through adoption.

There are many types of adoption, including legal, informal, open, semi-open, closed, domestic, transracial, and transnational. Legal adoption is when the process of taking on the responsibility of raising, parenting, or being the guardian of another person, often a young person, is formalized and documented by a government or other institution. Informal adoptions are those that may not be formally recognized in the way that legal adoptions are, but this does not make them "illegal." Depending on the surrounding laws and the individual circumstances, the biological family of an adoptee may continue contact with the adoptee throughout their lives in something called an open or semi-open adoption. Whether due to safety, privacy, or personal considerations, an adoption may be closed, where information about the biological relatives is kept confidential from the adoptee, and vice versa. A domestic adoption is when someone is adopted within the country they were born, and an international adoption is when someone is adopted from a different country, which would also make the adopted person a transnational adoptee. In the case where a child or minor is temporarily or permanently removed from the care of their parents or guardians, there is *foster care*, which is a system in which a government institution appoints a caretaker or guardian to a minor. Sometimes these caretakers are called foster parents. Children are sometimes adopted out of foster care, while others may live in foster care until they reach legal adulthood without being adopted. It is impossible to know why someone is placed into foster care or on the path toward adoption without asking, and we must keep in mind that we are not entitled to this information even if we are curious. Take note that it is archaic and disrespectful to use the word *orphan* or to assume that every person in foster care or on the path to adoption, is without parents. If someone self-describes as an "orphan," that is valid and should not be policed. My mom's adoption was a domestic closed adoption at birth, which means she was raised in the same country (and in her case, the same community, in Southern California) as her biological family. But her biological family (beyond her birth mother) was not informed of her existence. Ironically, she grew up around people she was related to, but didn't learn this until she reconnected with them in adulthood.

My grandparents, a Jewish Romanian American man and a Black American woman, sought to adopt children who looked as though they were their birth children, so my mother was rarely asked if she was adopted. My mother and my uncle, who are both adopted and not biologically related, are racialized as mixed (having Black and European ancestry), so they resembled what one might imagine my grandparents' biological offspring to look like. Adoptions are not always carried out this way, however. Many people choose transracial adoptions, which is when an adoptee and their adoptive family come from different racialized or ethnic backgrounds. (We'll discuss race and racialization in chapter 5.) Often, transracial adoptees and their parents may not resemble each other. Whether or not we are adopted, we do not always look like the people who raise us. Making offhand remarks about whether someone resembles their parents or caregivers can be harmful, disrespectful, and unnecessary. Genetic variation may cause us to look completely different from the people we are related to. So, making assumptions about resemblance reveals a limited and inaccurate understanding of family.

Growing up, the only parents my mother knew were the people who raised her. As an adult, she made the decision to seek out her biological family in order to satisfy her lingering curiosity about the people she came from. It is sometimes assumed that people seek out their birth families because their adoptive families were "not enough," or that their life was "incomplete" without this information. The reasons why someone chooses to pursue a reconnection with their biological relatives (or not) are ultimately personal, and we must get smarter about family by letting go of our assumptions and speculations about other people's lives, particularly when these assumptions are based on biases and not direct information.

My mother was able to find and get in touch with her birth family—who were not aware of her existence—with the help of a private investigator. It turned out that many of her birth relatives believed she had been stillborn (had died before being born). They had no idea that my mother was alive until she approached them as an adult with her own children, hoping to form a relationship. Through these new familial connections, my mother not only learned who her birth family was, but also that she was the result of a relationship between her biological mother and a man that she was not married to. The taboo of having a child with someone to whom you were not married was exacerbated by the fact that my birth grandmother was a white woman and my birth grandfather was a Black man. Two children resulted from their relationship. My birth grandmother was given an ultimatum by her husband: "I'll help you raise one, but not both." So, my mother was put up for adoption and didn't connect with her birth family for decades. But the relationships she has been able to have with her birth family are just as important to her as the relationships she has with people from her adopted family.

TOXIC FAMILY RELATIONSHIPS

In human societies throughout history, the family structure has helped people survive, as well as helped perpetuate legacies and traditions. The historical roots of "family" and the blueprints for it seen in the media can lead us to assume that everyone is part of a family, regardless of whether they actually participate in a familial relationship or not. Viewed from one perspective, this understanding may be a positive one, since an unconditional connection can be a beautiful, powerful thing. However, this understanding of family can also result in the expectation that we should subject ourselves to harmful and toxic behavior from people just because we live with them or are related to them.

Many of us might know someone (or be that someone) who does not have an ongoing relationship with the members of what others would consider to be their family. They may be described in formal terms as being "estranged," meaning that there is no longer a close or affectionate relationship. The reasons vary for why someone might be distant toward, estranged from, or not in contact with members of their family, including familial rejection, abuse, or social, political, or religious differences. For example, when I was in college, many of my friends decided to stay on campus instead of going back home over the holidays because their families did not accept them as openly LGBTQ+ individuals. In these circumstances it is completely valid to not have a relationship with the people you are related to, if they have chosen to be biased against you instead of respecting you. Sometimes it can be the healthiest and safest option for someone to cut off contact with their family members. It's also not uncommon for people to be estranged from certain family members but not others. For example, someone might not be on good terms with their parents, but be in touch with their siblings, or vice versa. We do not need to know why someone does not have a close connection to those we would call their family (nor do we have the right to ask about it), but we should remember not to assume that our familial contexts are the same as others.

It's often said that you can choose your friends, but you can't choose your family. And while it is true we can't retroactively choose the people we are born to, it is incorrect to say that the only family we can ever have are the people we are biologically related to. In many communities, it is commonplace to have siblings, parents, aunts, uncles, and auncles (a nonbinary portmanteau) who are not biologically related to us. This demonstrates that you certainly can choose your family in terms of how you engage in relationships with the people you are connected to in various contexts. The people we call family (whom we may not be biologically related to) are often called our "chosen family," and our chosen family is no less important or legitimate than our family of origin. Redefining our understanding of family is important because it validates "nontraditional" family structures and reminds all of us that we deserve healthy family relationships.

When members of a family choose to participate in oppressive ideologies like homophobia and transphobia, the result is often a rejection of their LGBTQ+ relative. It is imperative to remember that people who are impacted by oppression are not at fault for that oppression, nor are they required to forgive it and continue to experience its harms. Homophobia and transphobia place the expectation upon LGBTQ+ people that we should hide ourselves to avoid rejection and/or accept abusive and toxic treatment in order to belong. No one deserves, or should have to tolerate or experience, being in an environment that is harmful to their emotional or physical wellbeing. Unfortunately, for LGBTQ+ young people and other individuals who are not able to remove themselves from these harmful environments, survival may look like remaining closeted or enduring harm in order to be sheltered, to finish schooling, or to simply survive. (We'll discuss this further in chapter 6.) Such situations can be painful and even dangerous, so it's important as an outsider not to pressure such people to come out to or take stands with their families, or to judge them for doing what they need to do to survive in a toxic home. In the cases where an individual is able to remove themselves from a harmful and toxic family relationship, that individual can create a new family composed of close friends and community.

FRIENDSHIP

When thinking and talking about relationships, we often focus on family relationships and intimate partnerships, but friendships are just as important. Friendships can be just as challenging, rewarding, and complicated to maintain and understand as familial and intimate relationships. We make friends for various reasons, including but not limited to wanting a sense of belonging or companionship, or to avoid isolation. There are many types of friendships, from acquaintances to work friends and friends of friends to deeply meaningful connections with people who are among our closest loved ones. Not every one of our friends will be a lifelong one, but the time we spend and experiences we share with our friends become part of our lives even if we grow apart.

I never learned how to make friends in the same way that I learned how to ride a bike, swim, or paint, yet friendship is a much more prominent aspect of my life than any of those activities. When I think back on what I learned in school, at home, and on TV about friendships, it was all very abstract. I still haven't figured out the elusive "friendship equation," but I have gotten smarter about friendships over the course of my life. When I was in elementary school, I thought I should be friends with every single person in my class, and that if I couldn't be, there must be something wrong with me. I considered every unfulfilled friendship the result of my own failures. Maybe I wasn't likable enough, interesting enough, or worthy enough. It was stressful and exhausting, and by middle school, I preferred to be alone with my iPod and teenage angst—or at least, I thought so at the time. In hindsight, it was very isolating, but I got to know myself quite well, and all the time I spent in the library during lunch served me well as someone who now writes books. Looking back, I can also understand that

I was actively choosing isolation instead of risking the worthwhile vulnerability that friendship sometimes requires. It is a beautiful thing to create new connections with people, and whether or not we can continue that connection is not always a matter of rejection, but I felt that it was when I was younger. In fearing rejection, I also feared friendship. When middle and high school classmates reconnect with me now, I am often surprised when they share positive memories of me and consider us to have been friends. Though I refused to believe it at the time, not only was I a friend, but I also had friends the entire time! But my insecurities prevented me from feeling confident in these connections.

Getting smarter about friendship means understanding that "friend" is a broad umbrella term for many different types of and levels of connection. What we consider to be our "friendship equation" may need to develop over the course of our lives, and may change as we change. With every friend we create a unique friendship. You may form a lifelong friendship from a single introduction, or one day become friends with someone you previously found irritating and intolerable. With friendship, all things are possible. From the starting place of ubuntu, friendship is a natural next step. Mutual respect and shared humanity are the baseline for human interactions, and friendship may evolve from this to include mutual interests, differing interests, shared contexts, and more. The goal of a healthy friendship is not to become the same person as your friend, but to remain individuals while also building a relationship made from equal contributions that is maintained and repaired as life's changes and challenges affect the relationship. Friendship is not only about consistently demonstrating respect, trustworthiness, kindness, and active participation, but also about creating a space for you and your friends to grow. Whether that growth brings you closer together or further apart is not the defining factor of whether a friendship is successful.

I finally started to open myself up to friendships during college. I made the decision to attend Louisiana State University (LSU), where I was certain

I would not come across anyone from my hometown, and very few people even from my home state of California. Being away from all the people I knew allowed me to be my full self and not worry about embarrassing myself or my family. At such a massive school, with over 35,000 students, I could meet 100 people in one day and never see them again. It was the perfect training ground for infinite friendships. Instead of gradually forming an organic friendship, I would simply ask someone, "Would you like to be friends?" And it worked! I met my two best friends at LSU.

When I entered the workforce, my childhood expectation of being friends with every single classmate transformed into an expectation of being best friends with every single coworker. This idea was influenced by the media's portrayal of coworker relationships, which made it seem as though friendship was a necessary aspect of any professional relationship. Of course, I learned this is not true and that it's entirely possible and common to have functional, respectful work relationships with people who are not also your personal friends. Not being friends with someone doesn't mean we're enemies; it may just mean that we're friendly with them, but they are otherwise an acquaintance. It's especially important to keep this in mind in the workplace because we end up spending a lot of time with our coworkers. Assuming a working relationship is also a friendship could lead us to try to become closer to a coworker than they are comfortable with. This is not always inappropriate, but it can be awkward and create expectations that others are not prepared for. It took me a long time to muster the courage to reject my coworkers' invitations to after-work drinks because I was concerned that I would be perceived as unfriendly or not a team player. We all come from different contexts, and it's important to communicate our expectations and boundaries. This prevents us from disappointing people and has helped me to manage my fears around rejection. I still struggle with this sometimes, but practice helps.

The rise of social media has also changed how we think about friendship and our connections with other people. Your mom, your coworkers, your ex, your barber, and someone you met once at a concert can now all be your "friends" online, whether or not you have a friendship or meaningful connection with them offline. That said, it's important to recognize that the relationships we create and sustain through online connections are valid, whether or not they extend beyond the online realm. At least half of the friendships I've had in my life have been formed and sustained through social media. As long as we form our online relationships safely, social media and the internet can be a great way to meet and connect with people. It is beautiful to be part of an online community. But at the same time, it's important to remember that the same guidelines that we've discussed about making friends at the workplace and at school apply to online friendships. A friendship can only be formed if both parties are clearly communicating, willing, and consenting participants upon the embarking of said friendship. Social media complicates this because you can easily follow or add a "friend," but this isn't the same thing as communicating to someone you know that you'd like to create a meaningful friendship. Following someone on social media may be an important step in maintaining a friendship with someone, depending on the situation, but other important factors must come into play.

Like all good relationships, friendship takes work, but that work is well worth the camaraderie we gain. Active participation and reciprocal acts are what sustain a friendship. We may become friends with someone because we grew up in the same neighborhood or went to the same school. I call these friendships "circumstantial friendships," because they are based on a shared circumstance or context. In fact, most of our friendships are based on shared circumstances, and this does not invalidate them in any way. But shared circumstances alone can't always sustain a friendship without effective communication and participation from both people. Strong connections, compatibility, vulnerability, and mutual interests and values sustain friendships in ways that can't necessarily be achieved simply by coming from the same neighborhood or community. Yet for some people, being from the same neighborhood or community may be enough to spark and sustain a lifelong friendship. All friendships are unique. Engaging in friendships with purpose and intention doesn't always mean communicating on a daily, weekly, or even monthly basis, but it does mean that when you reconnect with someone you consider to be your friend that you do so with purpose and intention. How often you communicate with your friends depends on the individual relationship and the individuals in that relationship.

In intimate partnerships, there is often a discussion about how to define the relationship—the "What are we to each other?" talk—that is not common in friendships. Interrupting the "flow" of a growing relationship by asking what you should call it may feel unnatural, but it can be a helpful step to avoid any misunderstandings or assumptions. Defining our friendships can also help us to determine and reaffirm what we like about them and why we are in them. Simply letting someone know you are grateful for their friendship is a good way to indicate your feelings about the relationship, and may also invite the other person to express their feelings. In circumstances where it might be awkward to ask someone, "Are we friends?" you may be able to rely on indirect indications that you are indeed friends or getting closer to someone—for example, because they continue to reach out to you, invite you places, or accept your invitations to activities. Discussing your friendship can help to remove doubt and establish what steps you can take to reach the coveted status of "best friend." You may have more than one best friend in your life and more than one best friend at a time. What a best friend is to you might be different from what a best friend is to me. With time, trust, and similar interests, a friend can become a best friend.

Part of adulthood for me has been recognizing when I am trying to create a friendship when one is not welcome or available. This is slightly different from being rejected outright, because the other person might not overtly say "I don't want to be friends." Instead, they may choose to keep the relationship more casual or otherwise make it clear that they don't want the same level of connection I do. It can *feel* like rejection, though. If you can't have a friendship (or the level of friendship you want) with someone, that's okay. There are many reasons why people might not be interested in being friends, and those reasons may not be about you. Especially as people grow into adulthood and take on an expanding list of personal, familial, and professional commitments, it can be challenging to form new friendships or invest in deepening more casual relationships. The good news is that there are plenty of other people in the world who want and need friends. We are all potential friends to each other if we decide to be.

Getting smarter about friendship means recognizing that friendship is a reciprocal relationship that requires active participation. With ubuntu as the basis for all our interactions with our friends, we have the unique opportunity to share ourselves with others and grow together through shared experiences and a steadfast camaraderie. If you're seeking more friends, remember that to make and keep a friend, you must be a friend.

INTIMATE PARTNERSHIPS

Intimate partnerships are relationships involving some level of intimacy. This can encompass many things, including having mutual interests, living together, and/or sharing responsibilities that may be formalized. Intimacy may also include physical things like hugging, kissing, hand holding, other forms of touch, or simply being in close proximity to someone. Depending on the context and participants, intimacy may or may not be sexual in nature. Like all relationships, intimate partnerships and the interactions within them should be based on mutual respect, trust, compassion, and consent in order to be healthy. Sometimes intimate partnerships indicate the status of the relationship with labels such as "partners," "girlfriends," "boyfriends," "joyfriends," "fiancés," "spouses," and others. There are many different types of intimate partnerships, and we will get smarter about the diverse ways that people form these types of relationships.

When it comes to relationship structures that may be different from what we are used to seeing, we may inappropriately pass judgment or demonstrate our own biased assumptions. In some cases, we may be socialized to believe that some relationships are inherently harmful, while others are inherently good. In some cases, this is true, like predatory relationships between adults and children or relationships lacking fundamental aspects like consent and respect—both are inherently harmful. One of the best ways to get smarter about intimate relationships is to learn the different ways they can be structured. *Monogamous* means being in an intimate partnership with one individual. *Polyamorous* means forming intimate partnerships with more than one person at a time, with the knowledge and consent of all participants in the relationship. Monogamy, which is sometimes also called *monamory*, is often understood through the lens of a marriage or a long-term commitment to a single partner (though of course, not all marriages or long-term partnerships are monogamous). In the United States, the terms *polyamory* and *polygamy* are not used interchangeably like *monogamy* and *monamory* are. Polygamy, which comes from the roots *poly* (many) and *gamy* (marriage), specifically refers to marriage to more than one partner simultaneously and is criminalized in the United States and widely viewed as morally incorrect regardless of whether the parties have consented. The stigma associated with polygamy is why that term is not used interchangeably with polyamory. While not against the law, polyamorous relationships are also often socially stigmatized, though this is changing as more people become aware of this relationship structure. The bottom line when it comes to relationship structures is that a monogamous relationship is not inherently healthier, better, or safer than a polyamorous one. The idea that monogamy is the correct and only form of intimate partnership is supported by various institutions including legal and religious ones, which can make it difficult for people to understand or accept polyamorous partnerships. However, as long as polyamorous relationships are based in the requisite elements of healthy relationships (mutual respect, trust, consent, compassion), there's no need to pass moral judgments on them.

While the root word -*gamy* in *monogamy* specifically refers to marriage, monogamous partners don't need to be married for their relationship to be legitimate, and married people don't need to be monogamous for their marriage to be valid. People choose to get married—or not—for a variety of reasons, including personal considerations, religious beliefs, and practical factors. In most countries, legal protections are extended to individuals whose relationships are codified through marriage, which in many ways can be problematic and in other ways can make sense. In the case of anti-LGBTQ+ bias and prejudice, those who are unequivocally against same-gender relationships may incorrectly believe that a same-gender relationship will never be as valid or fulfilling as a heterosexual one. In this case, bias prevents prejudiced people from recognizing that regardless of the gender of the participants, if intimate partnerships are based on love, trust, consent, and compassion, that is ample reason to respect and honor them. Personal beliefs rooted in bias can also influence laws and policies. In 1996, President Bill Clinton signed the Defense of Marriage Act into law, which defined marriage as being only between a man and a woman (a heteronormative structure). In 2012, this homophobic legislation was repealed, making marriage something that any two people can enter into.

Many people (myself included) struggle with the idea of participating in an institution such as marriage that has such a fraught and problematic history as it relates to patriarchy, heteronormativity, and the concept of ownership. But getting smarter about relationships means understanding that all intimate partnerships, including marriage, can be redefined outside of institutional and societal definitions—they belong to the people in the relationship. As we understand the history of such institutions, we can analyze them and decide whether or not to engage with them based on what aligns with each of us and our values.

ABUSIVE RELATIONSHIPS

When relationships and partnerships lack mutual respect, trust, compassion, and consent, they may become unhealthy, toxic, and abusive. There are many ways that a relationship can be unhealthy, and this is not always indicated by arguments or disagreements. It is natural to disagree at times, and even argue, because the exchange of differing ideas and information is a part of being human and being in human relationships. How we communicate about, address, and resolve conflict is what defines what is and isn't healthy. It can sometimes be difficult to identify a toxic relationship, especially when it is our first intimate partnership, or if we haven't seen or experienced a relationship built on mutual respect. An unhealthy or unsafe relationship may even begin as a healthy one. When a relationship becomes toxic, there is usually a combination of subtle and overt actions that build over time and become cyclical in nature. Warning signs include mental and emotional manipulation like gaslighting, which can take many forms, but is typically characterized by someone dismissing our feelings, denying our shared reality, downplaying instances in which harm was caused to us or others, and manipulating information for the purposes of causing us to doubt our own perceptions. Abuse is cyclical, and often occurs in the following stages.

- **CALM:** No abuse is actively occurring.
- **TENSION:** Abuse feels imminent if the "wrong" thing is done or said.
- **INCIDENT:** Abuse occurs or is occurring.
- **RESTART:** Abuse is dismissed, justified, or apologized for (which may include excuses, gifts, or gaslighting of the survivor by the abuser).

Interpersonal violence can take many different forms including physical, emotional, sexual, and financial abuse. Depictions of abuse sometimes exclusively focus on physical and sexual violence, but it's important to remember that any instance where an interaction is based on coercion and not consent is a harmful one. The primary indication of whether or not a relationship is a healthy one is the role of consent. *Consent* is another word for "permission," and it is necessary to indicate a person's willingness to participate in an activity, event, or experience. Consent is fundamental to all relationships. It can feel very awkward to ask for consent every step of the way in a relationship or interaction, but doing so is necessary because it demonstrates respect for the other people in our relationships and is the only way to know whether or not someone wants to participate in a shared experience. This is especially crucial because underlying social dynamics like sexism, racism, ableism, and more may cause us to feel inappropriately and incorrectly entitled to other people's spaces and bodies.

The basis of consent is the recognition of individual bodily autonomy, meaning that your body belongs to you and no one else. Simultaneously, we do not have ownership over anyone else's body. This understanding of consent should be taught as early as possible and be reinforced throughout the various stages of life. Consent is applicable to every interaction, from whether or not you want a hug to whether or not you want to hold someone's hand. In the United States and many countries, there is a legal "age of consent" for different activities at different ages. This is most commonly discussed in reference to the age at which we can consent to sexual interactions. If we are to best protect young people from predators and abusers, sexual and otherwise, society must place the responsibility on adults to refrain from predatory behavior. We should not hold children and young people responsible for avoiding predation. We should also avoid using victim-blaming language, which wrongly places responsibility on the potential subjects of predation, whether they self-describe as survivors or victims.

By understanding and getting smarter about healthy and abusive relationships, we can fight the stigma that silences people and prevents them from getting out of harmful and dangerous circumstances. We can create space for individuals to be open and seek help when they are in harmful relationships. Intimate partner violence thrives in any society that creates taboos instead of infrastructure to protect vulnerable people. It's crucial to get smarter about abusive relationships by being conscious of how we talk about relationships, particularly when we talk about relationship conflicts. Victim blaming is harmful because it reinforces the incorrect idea that survivors should "stop being victims," rather than the fact that abusers should be held accountable for their abuse. Placing blame, judgment, and shame around the "success" of a relationship creates the expectation for many of us that it's better to stay in, rather than leave, a harmful relationship. No one deserves to be subjected to abuse, harm, or violence in any form or at any time. Removing ourselves from toxic relationships is often the safest and healthiest option.

MAINTAINING RELATIONSHIPS

All relationships require some work in order to remain healthy and functional, with some relationships needing more or less maintenance than others. A relationship that starts out healthy may become toxic if it's not properly nurtured, while an unhealthy relationship can sometimes be healed with time, intention, and emotional investment. When it comes to a problematic relationship, the challenge is often to figure out if it can be healed, or if it is worth fixing. For a relationship to be maintained, its status must be assessed. If both people are actively contributing to a relationship, then it's reciprocal. If a relationship is one-sided, however, it's "unrequited," meaning one person is participating, but the other is not. This can happen for various reasons. There may have been a miscommunication, or the person who's not participating is experiencing something unrelated that makes it difficult for them to maintain the relationship. One thing that will quickly make any relationship unsustainable is assumptions, so it's important to ask questions about the state of a relationship instead of making assumptions about it. Relationships are what we make of them, and sometimes no one but the participants can decide whether or not forgiveness and healing are possible. By establishing boundaries, communicating consistently and honestly, being accountable, and extending forgiveness, relationships can be built and maintained to withstand life's challenges.

BOUNDARIES

Boundaries are the rules and guidelines that we set for ourselves within relationships. The word *boundary* often implies something spatial, but boundaries can apply to emotional and mental aspects of relationships as well as physical limits. Boundaries are foundational to personal autonomy, privacy, and well-being, as well as to respect and consent in our relationships with others. For example, many of us have social anxiety and may struggle with being in large gatherings or meeting new people. If you are inviting someone to join you at a large event where they might not be comfortable, make sure you respect and accommodate their boundaries by being considerate of what they might need—for example, a designated space to decompress from the stimulation or confirmation that a familiar group of people will be there. Share information about the situation in advance so they can be prepared or make the best decision. It is important to get smarter about boundaries by remembering that when someone sets a boundary—such as ultimately choosing not to come to your event—it is not a personal attack or an indication that they don't trust us. On the contrary, it is an opportunity to establish trust when someone tells us what they need from us to feel respected, safe, and honored. Boundaries are personal and reflect the fact that we know what we need to feel secure. Healthy relationships allow for boundaries to be expressed and respected.

The most important thing when it comes to boundaries is to respect them, and a crucial part of this is accepting that we don't have to understand *why* a boundary exists in order to respect it. For example, if someone doesn't want a hug or doesn't generally like to be hugged, that boundary must be honored, and it's irrelevant—not to mention none of our business—why that person has that boundary. I may have different personal boundaries than you, and that's absolutely valid—personal boundaries are *personal* for that very reason. When we are expected to allow people into our personal space because "everyone else does" or it's "traditional" that is a fallacy of peer pressure that denies individuals the ability to set the boundaries for their interactions and to consent or decline those interactions. Even if we've been in a relationship for a long time, it is healthy and important to explicitly ask for consent instead of assuming. Consent can be given in different ways, and one of the clearest ways is with an enthusiastic, affirmative verbal communication, like "Yes." Importantly, not everyone communicates by speaking, and consent can also be expressed with body gestures like nodding one's head, giving a thumbs-up, or moving forward with an activity (which varies depending on the activity). Even if we said yes or initially consented to something, we can always change our mind and say no, and that "no" should be respected.

If actively establishing and reinforcing boundaries is new to you, it can feel awkward or uncomfortable at first, but it is an important part of maintaining relationships. We set boundaries for others in our lives about small things all the time—for example, we may be very firm with our friends about not telling us spoilers about a new movie or show that we haven't gotten the chance to see. We frequently set these boundaries with ease, whether it is blocking someone on social media or informing others of our food allergies. However, we may be hesitant to express our boundaries as confidently when they relate to our privacy, autonomy, well-being, and respect. Whether or not we can trust someone often depends on how well and consistently that person respects our boundaries. We cannot always establish these boundaries when we first meet someone, and our boundaries may change over the course of a relationship. It takes practice to build up the confidence to communicate boundaries, but it is an important skill to develop. Expressing a boundary with direct communication like saying, "I don't want a drink," when offered alcohol is not always respected or well received. In some cases, it can escalate the interaction from a casual conversation to a confrontation. While we shouldn't have to explain our boundaries, it is often helpful to use humor or rehearsed one-liners to avoid the onslaught of peer pressure that sometimes follows when our personal boundaries do not align with social expectations. In circumstances like being street harassed or "cat called," reinforcing the boundary that we do not want to communicate with the stranger might not be as explicit as saying, "I don't know you. This is a one-sided interaction and I am uncomfortable. Leave me alone." And that's okay. When there are unequal power dynamics or variables that we cannot account for, we should keep in mind that not reinforcing a boundary isn't a personal failure so long as we are able to remain safe and secure.

Unfortunately, social and peer pressures are major factors in the boundaries we feel comfortable setting. Often there are expectations associated with relationships that are not dictated by the people in the relationship, but by society or a peer group. These are known as "social boundaries," "social expectations," or "social norms," and are the rules and guidelines society sets about how we as individuals should and should not interact with one another virtually, physically, emotionally, and mentally. Like many things created by society at large, these expectations rarely work well for everyone.

There are often elements of bias incorporated into social boundaries just like there are elements of bias incorporated into society. In some places, social boundaries may prohibit public displays of affection, and these social boundaries might be codified into law. Anti-LGBTQ+ hate, for example, prevents same gender couples from being able to express affection publicly in the same manner that a heterosexual couple may be allowed. (Importantly, personal boundaries determine whether an individual consents to a public display of affection in the first place.)

Everyone deserves to have their boundaries respected, because we should be the ones who determine how others interact with us. Whether this is a new concept for you or you are practiced at setting boundaries, we can all get smarter about the boundaries we create for ourselves and how we respect the boundaries of others. Here is a list of steps that we can use in order to create and set personal boundaries:

1. Reflect on what you want and need from an interaction, circumstance, relationship or other situation in order to feel respected and secure.
2. Practice expressing these guidelines.
3. Express your boundaries.
4. Remind people of your boundaries (if possible) when they are not respected.

COMMUNICATION

Communicating, or exchanging information, is an essential part of all relationships because it allows us to express ourselves to the people we are connected with. Communication can happen in many ways and doesn't always have to be with speech—after all, not everyone communicates by speaking. Clear communication can be achieved in many forms such as sign language, sounds, body language, lip reading, tactile finger spelling, written language, and spoken and nonspoken language. Barriers to communication can include inaccessibility; not understanding the language, accent, dialect, cultural norms, context, or intention; bias; power dynamics; and more. When I dated a woman who was not an English speaker, we struggled to communicate effectively. Our only shared language was Spanish, which we both spoke with dubious proficiency, so we used translation software on our dates. Technology is not infallible, though, so of course we made some mistakes. Once I meant to convey that she was being clever and sneaky by keeping a surprise from me, but when I went to translate the word *sneaky*, the result in her first language (which I'm not sharing here to protect her privacy) was "thief-like." So instead of trying to convey my gratitude flirtatiously and playfully, I inadvertently insulted her by calling her dishonest. Not ideal at all! I had to figure out why she was frustrated when I was attempting to be playful, and it was a challenge to explain that it must have been a mistranslation and that calling her dishonest was not my original intention. When our sole communication method is language, we can lose important context that enriches our experience with people, which often leads to miscommunication. Context is very important, as is being patient and willing to troubleshoot when communication goes awry.

Technology has brought so many people together by bridging language gaps and isolation resulting from distance, ableism, and more, but communicating with written language such as text messages, social media posts, or even books can still be difficult. Whether this is because of different contexts, neurodiversity, or other factors, it is very common for our communications to be misinterpreted. Because of this, context tags, emojis, and internet shorthand like "LOL" have become popular methods of communicating tone and intent. For example, the phrase "I can't wait to get another email" may be understood as a genuine message of anticipation or as sarcasm. Adding a smiling emoji or the context tag /*gen* (for "genuine") can indicate if the statement is meant to indicate enthusiasm, while adding an eyeroll emoji or context tag like /*s* (for "sarcasm") can indicate if the tone is facetious. As an online educator and influencer, I communicate with many people who are just starting to learn about some of the subjects I teach, so I could hurt a lot of people's feelings if I were to take every question I receive as a sarcastic one instead of assuming positive intent with every communication. Assuming a positive intention (or at least a neutral one) is often a good thing to do when interacting with people for the first time. Instead of assuming that I am being trolled or mocked when someone asks me a question online, I assume that the person asking is genuinely unfamiliar with the content and seeking an earnest answer. A simple "Can you clarify what you mean?" or "Can you ask that differently?" has been an effective way for me to determine whether someone is being disrespectful or inquisitive. It also saves me the emotional labor of determining whether I should feel defensive or be receptive to the communication.

Even when there are no obvious communication barriers, communication can still be challenging, and difficult conversations are sometimes necessary. People may be anxious and apprehensive talking about taboo subject matter or when trying to express a feeling of being disrespected and/or violated. If you need to have a tough conversation, keep these six key principles in mind:

1. Start from a place of mutual respect.

2. Speak to share a message, not to change minds.

3. Be present and listen with intention. Avoid participating in the conversation to dismiss and silence the other participants.

4. Set boundaries and respect boundaries. Respect when or if the other person is ready to talk. Remember that tough conversations can happen in moments of calm instead of during hectic or intense moments.

5. Speak from your personal experience, not on behalf of others. Be open to reliable sources when discussing information that is not personal.

6. Be patient with yourself and others. Conversations do not need to be "won."

This road map can help us to prioritize how, when, and for what purpose we communicate something that might be difficult to talk about. As discussed in chapter 1's section on beliefs, it's key to consider when and if a belief we or others have is worth debating. If the belief is harmful and dehumanizing, it is absolutely okay to not engage with it. It's important for the difficult conversation framework to begin with mutual respect—understanding that even if there is disagreement, the parties in the conversation will respect one another and acknowledge each other's humanity. Attacking the other person or bringing up unrelated past behavior to avoid addressing the current moment's issue are common problems that arise when having a tough conversation. Take care not to deflect and distract from the current issue unless it is connected and relevant to the issue at hand. While these conversations may be difficult and uncomfortable, they are often necessary to allow us to communicate and maintain healthy relationships.

ACCOUNTABILITY AND APOLOGIZING

In the course of forming and maintaining relationships, we will inevitably make mistakes. If we violate an individual's boundaries, disrespect them, or otherwise do something that puts our trustworthiness in question, it is appropriate for us to take responsibility (or accountability) for that mistake. At some point we will be in positions where we must take accountability for a mistake made toward others, and at some point we will need to determine whether to forgive someone who has made a mistake toward us. Whether we decide to forgive someone may depend on if and how they apologize or demonstrate their accountability. When we do something that causes harm, it is important to remember that regardless of whether we intended to cause harm, if harm has been caused as a result of our actions, then we must take responsibility for our actions. Intention does not equal impact. Being responsible in this way may also be understood as recognizing being at fault.

As a child, I learned that taking accountability means apologizing by saying "I'm sorry." As I grew up, I saw how frequently someone would say "I'm sorry" in anticipation of the other person immediately extending forgiveness by saying "it's okay." But sometimes it's not okay. The word *sorry* comes from the Germanic root meaning "pained." "I'm sorry," depending on the region and the context can mean everything from "forgive me," to "excuse me," "I feel bad," "can you repeat yourself?" and more. If we've violated a boundary or otherwise harmed or disappointed someone, the most important thing isn't necessarily that we feel bad about it, but that we understand what we've done. We don't have to *feel* sorry to be sorry or to take accountability or responsibility and to do better in the future. The word *apology* comes from the Greek apologia, meaning "a speech in defense." In this historical context, apologia was a methodical response or justification for an allegation or accusations of wrongdoing. Ironically, the current understanding of what an apology is could not be further from this Greek origin. Apologies in the present context are statements of regret for an offensive, disrespectful, harmful, or disappointing action.

An apology may be necessary to rebuild trust, but without a statement of intention and a plan to do better in the future, it's hard to trust that someone will make amends and for us to determine whether or not to forgive them. Let's examine what it looks like to apologize through the following framework I developed while mediating conflict between students. Before making an apology, be honest with yourself about your intentions for apologizing. In many cases we may not be forgiven immediately or at all, so carefully consider your intention and your goal. Ideally, your goal is to take accountability and make reparations to the person you have harmed, whether they decide to forgive you. Here are four effective steps we can use to apologize:

1. Take responsibility for your actions that harmed the other person and the result of your actions. Accountability is key to rebuilding trust.

2. Apologize, making sure to focus your apology on how the other person was affected rather than how *you* were affected. This is a form of deflection and puts the other person in the position of having to address your feelings even though they are the one who has been harmed.

3. Express that you understand that what you did was harmful, disappointing, or offensive, and why. If what you are saying isn't in alignment with what the other person feels, then you may be able to discuss the issue further to come to a mutual understanding.

4. Communicate your intention or plan to do better in the future and how (if possible) you can repair the wrong.

Here's an example of what you might say to apologize for saying you would cook dinner and then not doing it.

1. "I didn't cook dinner even though I said I would."

2. "I'm sorry."

3. "I understand that you were counting on me to do this and I disappointed you."

4. "I am going to start cooking now, and next time I'm asked I will set an alarm so I don't lose track of time."

Your apology must begin with an acknowledgment of your accountability, demonstrate an understanding of the harm you caused, come from a place of humility, and include your intentions to be and do better in the future. Whether or not your apology is accepted often depends on how harmful your action was. Even if the only thing that will make things better is time, an apology is an important step to take to demonstrate your understanding, good intentions moving forward, and mutual respect.

REFLECTION QUESTIONS

- How do you define "family"?

- How do you define "chosen family"?

- What are some of your personal boundaries? Sometimes it can take practice to enforce these or figure them out.

- What does the concept of ubuntu mean to you? Discuss or journal about an example of "humanity toward others" and/or "I am because you are" in your life.

- Give some examples of healthy relationships in your life or in the media. What makes them healthy?

- What assumptions do people make about your family/relationships? What assumptions do you make about the family/relationships of others?

- How has your understanding of "friendship" evolved throughout your life?

- How do you feel about the boundaries in your relationships with your family, friends, and intimate partner (s)? Are there any boundaries you could work on developing and enforcing?

CHAPTER 3

GET SMARTER ABOUT CLASS

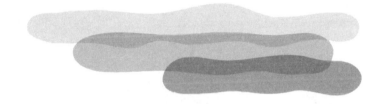

Social class, also known as socioeconomic status, is an underdiscussed but extremely important aspect of our social identities to get smarter about. *Socioeconomic* is a term that describes the interaction of social and economic factors. Our social class is usually determined by a combination of our actual or perceived education, income, wealth, occupation, and the associated prestige or stigma assigned to us within a society. This is often called "social standing," which illustrates how our perceived or actual social class is often used to determine our rank or position within society. It's important to emphasize the role of perception in understanding class because bias, discrimination, and prejudice are not based on facts or evidence, but on assumptions. In capitalist societies, including the United States, people with more capital (owned wealth in the form of money or other assets) are "higher class," and are valued more than people with less or no capital. *Capitalism* is an economic and political system in which trade and industry are controlled by private owners for profit. The framework of class in various economic theories like capitalism informs whom society views and treats as "valuable" and "worthy." *Classism* is the system of oppression that defines our worth or value based on our actual or our perceived social class. Mutual respect and recognition of our humanity should not have to be earned, but many of our institutions do not reflect this truth due to classism. Understanding class is crucial for getting smarter about every other aspect of identity and lived experience discussed in this book.

Eurocentric social structures are the basis of today's class systems in Eurocolonial countries. *Eurocentrism*, a term coined in the 1970s by Marxian economist and political scientist Samir Amin, is the prioritizing of European ideology, values, ethics, morality, and constructs while diminishing and erasing all others. The concept of "the Western world" is an example of Eurocentrism, since it positions Europe and North America as "the West," which is geographically relative. For the Indigenous peoples in Turtle Island, or the Americas, European colonizers came from the east. The idea of "the Western world" is rooted in European colonization, and social "progress" is incorrectly assessed accordingly. For this reason, it's accurate to say "Eurocolonial" when describing what is inaccurately known as "the West" or "Western world." When naming specific regions, use updated language such as Southwest Asia and North Africa (SWANA) instead of "the Middle East," and Asia (or the actual country names) instead of "the East" or even more archaically "the Orient." Combating Eurocentrism as we get smarter about class also means prioritizing the works of non-European economists and political theorists like Claudia Jones, Kwame Nkrumah, Cedric Robinson, and Julius Nyerere.

In the United States we are often separated into upper, middle, and lower classes, but in this chapter we will focus on the power dynamics created by class and economic theories that inform the creation of class in general. Social class is not determined in a vacuum—it is influenced by racism, sexism, ableism, and more. To get smarter about class, we must examine our understanding of labor and capitalism.

LABOR AND CLASS

After I graduated from college, I moved to Washington, DC, to attend the Howard University School of Law. My decision to go to law school was universally praised, but the experience itself was not what I expected. Instead of committing myself to something I could not tolerate for the next three years, I dropped out after only seven weeks. Dropping out was the right choice for me, but it was made more difficult by many of my friends and family members who dismissed and doubted my decision. It was during this time that I realized just how much emphasis we place on our relationship to work and education as it relates to our worth. This emphasis can be understood as *meritocracy*, or the political ideology that affords power, access, and influence to people based on perceived merit. *Merit* is a characteristic or action deserving of honor or esteem, and in theory, a meritocracy would reward those deemed most worthy due to their ability, skills, or work ethic rather than perpetuate a society ruled by those with the most access to power. The problem with a meritocracy is that what constitutes "merit" is deeply subjective and dependent on context. What our society deems honorable, worthy, and valuable is fundamentally based in ableism, racism, sexism, classism, and other systems of oppression.

I didn't have a plan when I dropped out of law school, but I knew I needed a source of income, so I joined a childcare agency and started working as a nanny and babysitter for a few DC families. The money was good, the work was fulfilling, the hours were flexible, and I was often asked to travel with the families on vacation at no expense to me. Thanks to classism however, I was quickly reminded that the way work is viewed socially is not only a matter of the wages we earn or the opportunities our work allows us, but the prestige or stigma assigned to *how* we earn our wages. When I would attend social and cultural events in DC on my days off, the question that immediately followed meeting a new person was "What do you do?" This question was never a philosophical one. It was the shorthand version of asking "What do you do for a living?" or "What is your job?" At the time, my job was being a nanny, so that was what I would answer. Almost every time, I would notice the eyes of the person I was in conversation with immediately glaze over with disinterest. People who were more interested in career connections than human connections would assume that I could not bring any value to a conversation or relationship. When I meet new people now and tell them I am an author and educator, I generally do not have that same experience. Because my work is "intellectual" or considered by society to be merited, my personhood is generally regarded by classist structures as having a higher value based solely on my work and corresponding perceptions. Importantly, I'm the same person, and am no more or less valuable as an author than I was as a nanny.

The work we do is usually described as labor, and not all labor is valued equally by society. Nor are all laborers viewed equally to each other because of the simultaneous role of other systems of oppression. Labor has generally been divided into a binary of skilled and unskilled work in Eurocolonial contexts, and modern understandings often describe labor as unskilled, semiskilled, skilled, and professional. All these definitions refer to how specialized the work is.

- **UNSKILLED LABOR:** not requiring special skills or training.
- **SEMISKILLED LABOR:** requiring some, but not extensive, skills or training.
- **SKILLED LABOR:** requiring special skills, training, knowledge, and ability.
- **PROFESSIONAL LABOR:** requiring extensive or advanced skills and education.

The word *skill* comes from the Old English word for "knowledge," and means an expertise or ability to do something well. This division of labor by "skill" values most the labor of the "highly educated" professional class, which within Eurocolonial society is made exclusive to white men with access to capital. Everyone is skilled at something, and usually more than one thing. However, these classifications of labor by skill level (which are compensated accordingly) have been defined almost exclusively by European and Eurocolonial perspectives, values, and philosophies. This compensation does not occur outside of oppressive factors, and it's not an accident that the labor that is generally considered to be unskilled or low skilled has historically been relegated to marginalized people. Those who are deemed less valuable by society are pushed into work that is deemed less valuable by society. Yet all work requires skill and knowledge, and all work should be fairly compensated and respected. Regrettably, this limited understanding commonly informs wages and salaries, and in many countries, it informs who may be granted a visa or citizenship. And because health care is tied to work in the United States, it can also dictate who has access to health insurance and health care.

Getting smarter about class means understanding the power dynamics connected to it, which requires an intersectional approach. *Intersectionality*, a term coined in 1989 by Dr. Kimberlé Crenshaw, is a framework that requires us to consider multiple forms of oppression at one time. In a racist patriarchy, without an intersectional framework, only white women would be considered under a sex and gender analysis and only Black men would be considered under a racial analysis. Keep in mind that intersectionality is not just us naming our identities, but also our context and the ways that systems of oppression either harm or benefit us accordingly, and we must include class analysis in addition to the many other aspects that make up our identities. Professor of gender, sexuality, and feminist studies Dr. Jennifer C. Nash highlights how intersectionality is not itself a tactic for fighting oppression, but is instead a lens through which anti-oppression tactics can be devised. When approaching our understanding of labor and work from an intersectional perspective, the gender and racial wage gap offers an apt example. In the United States,

March 24 is Equal Pay Day, or the number of days into a year it would theoretically take a white woman to work to make the same amount of money in a particular job as a white man had the previous year. So, for example, if a white man made $100,000 in one calendar year (365 days), a white woman impacted by the sexist wage gap would theoretically not make that same amount of money until March 24 of the following year (448 days). Simultaneously, the white man in this example would be 83 days into making his next $100,000. Black Women's Equal Pay Day is even later in the year in August, reflecting that Black women not only experience a sexist wage gap, but also a racist one. Other groups of racialized women also experience a racist and sexist wage gap. These inequalities reveal that compensation is not exclusively based on the type of labor, but is also informed by how society values and devalues the person doing that labor. Without this necessary context, we don't get a full picture of income inequality.

The fact that a white man is more highly compensated than a Black woman—with a Black woman making $0.48 to $0.68 to a white man's $1.00 in the US—is because of the white supremacy and patriarchy that the class system in the United States is built on. Economists project that the sexist wage gap will be closed by 2059 based on data showing that it has narrowed by $0.08 in the past 25 years. But this will only remedy the wage gap between white men and white women. The wage gap between white men and Black women can close sooner if the people in power create policies and laws to make it a priority. Policies like paid family leave, pay transparency, and redress for unfair hiring and promotion practices are all necessary steps that can be implemented to bring that projected parity year closer.

For people who cannot work or otherwise do labor in order to sustain themselves in a capitalist system, financial support programs like Social Security are meant to help. Like any system of oppression, classism is exacerbated by other forms of oppression like ableism. In the United States, eligibility for Supplemental Security Income (a financial support program that many disabled people depend on) places limits on the capital that participants are allowed to have. To be eligible in 2020, "your countable resources must not be worth more than $2,000 for an individual or $3,000 for a couple." As it says plainly on the government website, "We call this the resource limit," and countable resources include "anything else you own which can be changed to cash and used for food or shelter." Only a few key things do not count toward your resource limit as a participant of SSI. While the application of these regulations may vary by person and state, it is possible that if you have more than $2,000 in a savings account and/or in the form of other assets, you might no longer be eligible for this crucial financial support program. Resource limits are meant to restrict the usage of this program to people in the most dire financial need, but in practice the restrictions around SSI and similar programs can impoverish participants while claiming to support them. This is largely due to the ableism and classism in society that dehumanizes people who are unable to work or do labor or people who have been impoverished. According to the Center for American Progress, "These limits have not been updated in 40 years, thus pushing beneficiaries deeper into poverty every year." Forty years ago, $2,000 would be worth the equivalent of $6,281.82 today when adjusted for inflation, but the asset limits remain at the levels set in 1980. Disability scholars and advocates have called for the asset limits to be raised, but the ways in which these programs are regulated are strongly influenced by ableism and classism. Disabled people are not the only ones who are subjected to problematic restrictions set by institutions that supposedly have our best interests in mind. It is important to look critically at the eligibility requirements and access barriers for programs that claim to be created to support us.

Getting smarter about class means understanding that our worth and right to live *well* is not tied to whether we do labor, what kind of labor we do, or how productive we are at that labor. The Black Panther Party's 1966 Ten-Point Program titled "What We Want" included important aspects like "decent housing fit for the shelter of human beings," and "land, bread, housing, education, clothing, justice, and peace" among the top requirements for a more just and equitable society. All people deserve to be recognized as inherently worthy by virtue of our existence, and we should not be ranked in a hierarchy based on how much we contribute—or are perceived to contribute—to an economy or a society. A lawyer is not inherently more valuable than a childcare worker, and neither are more inherently valuable than someone who does not or cannot have a traditional wage-earning job. Who we are and how we are valued should not be tied to "what we do." These Eurocolonial definitions of class status, work, and worth are deeply rooted in oppression, and we are made to believe that they are the only way of understanding labor and ourselves. Of course, this is not the case. Many of the ways that we understand our own work and our relationship to work are informed by the fact that we live in—or are heavily influenced by—primarily capitalistic systems that prioritize productivity and profit over people. Capitalism is not the only form of social organization, nor is the United States a purely capitalist system. Let's examine the social and economic theory of capitalism.

CAPITALISM

We cannot get smarter about social class without examining the ways that economic theory informs our understanding of it. Economic theories not only connect to things like money, but also to beliefs about power and how power should be distributed or denied. This study of power is called *politics*. In the United States, capitalism is often venerated as the best economic theory, and it is the foundation of our economy. Capitalism advocates for trade and industry to be controlled by private owners for profit. Capitalism in its most extreme and perfected form is enslavement, which is the absolute exploitation of the worker to the absolute benefit of the capitalist (or owner).

While it may be a dominant economic theory in practice in the world today, capitalism is a relatively recent invention when considering all of human history. Before capitalism, most societies were based on communalism, which has been described as a "primitive" form of communism. (Note that the word *primitive* should be avoided, as it is Eurocentric—it considers Eurocolonial society to be the definition of modernity and progress, and is often used in Eurocolonial contexts to describe anything related to Indigenous or other racialized peoples.) *Communalism* is a political and economic theory based on the organization of society and ownership into small local communes or communities working toward united purposes like safety, security, and sustainability. Prior to capitalism in Europe, there was communalism and feudalism. Paying rent to a landlord is one of the many remnants of feudalism. *Feudalism* has different meanings in different historical and regional contexts, but European feudalism was based on the exchange of land and services, which included agricultural, military, and political support. However, socially destabilizing crises like the Bubonic plague of the 1300s and the Hundred Years' War (1337–1453) between France and England created economic and political instability. Simultaneously, the depleted population and resulting consequences placed an increased social emphasis on individual human rights, including the right to education for serfs and peasants (instead of just nobles). This chipped away at the foundation of feudalism. With the coinciding rise of racialized colonization from the 1400s onward, feudalism declined steadily. A mainstay of the new capitalist model was solidified by the founding of two international corporations: the British East India Company in 1600, followed swiftly by the Dutch East India Company in 1602. Capitalism dawned during the early European colonization period, and corresponded with the invention of race, which we will get smarter about in chapter 5.

While capitalism is the primary economic theory utilized to within the United States, we are not exclusively a capitalistic system. Social welfare programs within the education, housing, and health care sectors are founded firmly on theories of socialism, and many people would not be able to survive without them. However, not enough people are provided access to them. Thinking critically about class and the economic theories behind our understandings of class is necessary for us to imagine and work toward a more compassionate, just, and equitable world.

RACIAL CAPITALISM

The United States can be understood as a racial capitalist society, or what Black studies scholar Dr. Charisse Burden-Stelly calls "modern US racial capitalism," defined as a "racially hierarchical political economy" that is sustained by war, imperialism, militarism, dispossession, and "labor superexploitation." For example, in the United States until 1865, chattel enslavement, or the buying, selling, trading, inheriting, and ownership of enslaved African people as property, defined and sustained the economy. Chattel enslavement is an example of labor superexploitation because it completely exploits the enslaved person and completely benefits the owner or capitalist.

Contemporary examples of racial capitalism and the requisite labor superexploitation include the crisis of mass incarceration that disproportionately impacts Black and other racialized people in the United States. At the time of writing, prison labor sustains many major companies like 3M, which had a net worth of $101 billion in 2020. Insourcing, or manufacturing products using prison labor, allows companies to state that their products are made in the USA (a claim that sometimes carries the assumption that worker rights are protected) while underpaying incarcerated people a reprehensible $0.23 to $1.15 per hour for the exact same work done by nonincarcerated people. In the United States, this is considered to be constitutional because the Thirteenth Amendment only abolished slavery and involuntary servitude "except as a punishment for crime." To best illustrate the superexploitation of prison labor, UNICOR, the government program that allows corporations to benefit from the labor of prisoners, reports that "inmates receive approximately $0.04 of each $1.00 in sales revenue, primarily used to repay important financial obligations." This data is used as the value proposition to companies seeking to use UNICOR prison labor in their supply chain. The fact that prisoners potentially only see four cents of every dollar is the reason companies that utilize prison labor are able to boast such massive profits. Wealth in this case comes at the expense or superexploitation of others. These wages, while inadequate, are often preferable to the meager $0.12 to $0.40 per hour for mandated prison work assignments like "food service, plumbing, painting, or groundskeeping" required of all "medically able" prisoners.

When we examine capitalism and the consequences specific to racial capitalism, we can get smarter about important injustices like impoverishment in an intersectional manner. Consider the disproportionally high number of unhoused people within the Black community or the disproportionally low number of Black people who are homeowners. In 2019, Black Americans accounted for 40 percent of all unhoused people in the United States, despite only comprising 13 percent of the US population (while white people accounted for 48 percent of all unhoused people in the United States and comprised 77 percent of the US population). In terms of housing, which we also explore in chapter 5, just 44 percent of Black American families own their own homes, compared with 73.7 percent of white American families.

Getting smarter about class helps us to see that the United States was built on and is sustained by the injustices of classism, racism, and other forms of oppression and discrimination. Throughout my public school education, I was taught about the wonders of capitalism and free markets. While capitalism, in theory, allows for free enterprise and unbridled growth and success through hard work, because of the class system and other forms of oppression, hard work does not automatically translate into capital under capitalism (as we can see plainly with the example of prison labor). For that to be a possibility, all labor or work would have to be valued equally and we would have to have regulations that codify and enforce that equal valuation. Much like feudalism, the people tilling the land or making the products benefit the least from their labor under capitalism, while the company leaders or owners benefit the most. Political and economic theorist Dr. Cedric Robinson's approach to the intersection of capitalism and racism examines how the social, cultural, political, and ideological complexes of European feudalism continue to the present day. In many cases, the benefits of capitalism are only beneficial because of the superexploitation of other people.

SOCIALISM

Socialism is often viewed as the opposite or antithesis of capitalism, but in reality, it is simply another way to think about economics and politics. Socialism advocates for community or social—rather than private—regulation of production, distribution, and exchange of capital. It prioritizes all members of a society as opposed to just a ruling few, with all things created by that society being distributed to benefit all members of that community. It's important to note that socialism and communism, while related, are not the same thing. Communism is the organization of society *without* private property, class divisions, and labor divisions. Socialism is often considered to be the bridge between communism and capitalism because it is the organization of society based on *limited* private ownership, class divisions, and labor divisions. The primary difference between capitalism and socialism is whether profit is privately or collectively owned and regulated.

Throughout United States history, capitalism and socialism have been pitted against each other as opposing forms of not only economic and social theory but also morality. The US's founding emphasis on private ownership (which fundamentally included the ownership of people via chattel slavery) has resulted in deep institutional and social biases against any form of economic theory that advocates for community ownership instead of private ownership. Throughout the twentieth century, calling someone a "communist" meant questioning their allegiance to the United States, and much of that prejudice lingers. In such instances, it didn't matter whether someone was a socialist or a communist, because these distinct theories were conflated and detested.

The social attitudes against communism and socialism were not exclusive to interpersonal contexts, but were a matter of US policy for decades. The House Un-American Activities Committee was created in 1938 to investigate alleged disloyalty and subversive activities by US citizens, public employees, and organizations suspected of having communist beliefs or ties to communist governments. The United States also worked to destabilize democratically elected communist and socialist governments, such as the US involvement in the Chilean coup d'état in 1973 against politician Salvador Allende. It is impossible to examine socialism without looking at this underlying context of institutional bias, and it's important to acknowledge that underlying apprehensions stemming from this bias can make this conversation a difficult one to have.

Just as capitalism works differently in various historical, regional, and circumstantial contexts, socialism also has many forms and applications. In 2019, the Pew Research Center found that 55 percent of people in the United States had a negative view of socialism, and only 42 percent had a positive view. The concerns around socialism included the ideas that it removes the incentive for people to work and be self-reliant and that it undermines democracy. Many of these fears are based in Cold War–era assumptions and myths instead of evidence-based examples of socialist implementation. Even with socialist programs like universal basic income (which provides a steady income to constituents based on surpluses of income from the economy), people still work, but people who do not or cannot work are, importantly, not penalized or impoverished. During the COVID-19 pandemic, stimulus checks effectively functioned as universal basic income for eligible United States citizens. Instead of collapsing the economy, these payments sustained it, and people who had jobs and could work continued to do so.

As for whether socialism undermines democracy, in some cases, democracy is actually reinforced by socialist public services. Any government program offering a socially funded service to any member of that society is socialist and "evidence that democracy works," according to performance studies and national security scholar Akeem Omar Ali. In the United States, a cherished fixture of our infrastructure is the United States Postal Service. The Postal Service is a socialist program, and despite the fact that only 42 percent of US citizens approve of socialism, 91 percent approve of the Post Office. This is why we must get smarter about socialism outside of biases and misinformation. As we covered in chapter 1 when we talked about beliefs, it's crucial to be open to well-researched information, even when it is contrary to ideas we have previously held by using critical thinking. For the cost of a stamp, our mail will be delivered, whether it is a check from an employer, Supplemental Security Income, a new credit card, or a mail-in ballot. The 2020 US presidential election could not have happened during the COVID-19 pandemic without the socialist program that is the Post Office.

Despite people's low approval of socialism in the United States, examples of it can be found everywhere. One socialist program many young people benefit from is the National School Lunch Program, which provides free or low-cost lunches to schoolchildren every day, and the Free Breakfast Program, which became popular following its widespread implementation in the US by the Black Panther Party in the 1960s, '70s, and '80s. Young people require nourishment to learn and thrive, and if a young person or their family cannot pay for daily lunches, that child should not go hungry. At some schools, the free lunches for students who cannot afford them are paid for by a surcharge on those students who can pay for lunch. In other cases, public school lunch programs may be funded by the government through taxes. Other examples of social or communal resource distribution include little libraries, community gardens, community fridges, and mutual aid funds. These community-organized initiatives help to offset problems like the lack of a publicly funded library (another socialist program) or food deserts resulting from the discriminatory redlining practices implemented during the Cold War era in the United States (which we will get smarter about in chapter 5). Caring for others in our community is a good thing, and many socialist programs allow us to fulfill this value.

One critique of socialism is the claim that it always fails. But what constitutes a failure or a success is dependent upon context and the power dynamics that dictate who declares the success or the failure. People in power whose wealth comes at the expense of others often consider socialism to be a threat to their power and wealth—and to be fair, it is. It is also a threat to systemic inequality, which enables wealth to be hoarded at the expense of the people who are impoverished by that hoarding. In socialism, if a person's livelihood comes at the expense of other people's lives, that oppression would be accounted for through things like policies and taxes. Being taxed is not remotely the same as facing the impacts of impoverishment and exploitation. In socialistic countries there are still millionaires and billionaires, but they pay their fair share in taxes instead of exploiting tax breaks that enable them to hoard wealth without giving back to the system that allowed them to earn it (which we will get smarter about in the next section).

Racial capitalism is considered to be immensely successful by millionaires and billionaires, but for incarcerated people making less than a dollar an hour to produce products that make those millionaires and billionaires wealthy, it is an abject failure. When equality looks more like a failure than success and progress, it may be because we are too encumbered by privilege to think critically about the ways some people's dreams are made possible by other people's nightmares. As civil rights organizer and Pan-Africanist Kwame Ture declared, "Every economic system must answer one fundamental question: who will own and control the wealth of the country? The question can only be answered in two ways: either a few will own, or everyone will own. It's as simple as that." His analysis requires us to continue working toward a more intentional, informed, and compassionate society. As explained by political theorist and Pan-Africanist Kwame Nkrumah, there must be a shift in the ethics surrounding capitalism in order for us to have socialism or any form of economic organization that does not prioritize individual people making profits at the expense of the larger society.

Economic theories, whether based on private or public ownership, have been used with wide-ranging efficacy throughout history up to the present day. If we don't examine the systems of social and economic organization that govern our lives, we risk falling victim to their worst elements while only learning about their best ones. Getting smarter means determining which aspects of our understanding need to be challenged as well as expanded.

WEALTH HOARDING VS. COOPERATIVE ECONOMICS

A capitalist system fundamentally creates enormous wealth disparities, in which some people don't have enough resources to survive, while others amass and hoard far more resources than they need or could reasonably use in a single lifetime. Since people in power have economic as well as social and political authority, many of our institutions are designed to uphold, obscure, or praise this massive inequality. During the COVID-19 pandemic that began in 2020, billionaire business magnates Jeff Bezos and Elon Musk made unfathomable profits despite the havoc the pandemic inflicted on the economy and society at large. The economic downturn, health care crisis, and housing crisis exacerbated by the pandemic meant that people around the world suffered without access to basic human needs such as food, housing, and health care. While the pandemic didn't create this chasm between the haves and have-nots, such stark consequences can help us get smarter about wealth hoarding. As of this writing, Elon Musk has hoarded so much capital that he could spend $500,000 every day for the next 100 years and not run out of money.

In order for billionaires or a few ridiculously wealthy people to exist, they must hoard resources in the form of capital at the expense of everyone else. In 2018, the top 1 percent of US taxpayers had an average annual income of $1,316,985, while the average income for everyone else (the 99 percent) was just $50,107. Without getting smarter about wealth hoarding, it is difficult to fully capture just how many resources are being held by a minuscule percentage of people in the United States. From a capitalist standpoint, any decision that results in workers being paid more money for their labor is considered to be a "bad business decision" unless it results in more productivity or more profits. In a capitalist system, the people who sell their work for wages (like myself) are called workers (or "the 99 percent"), and the people who benefit the most from that labor are called capitalists (or "the 1 percent"). Capitalism encourages employers to pay their workers the bare minimum (in other words, the literal minimum wage), and the US government allows these companies to spend a percentage of their income to lobby or influence political leaders to pass laws in the interest of corporations. Unions, or organizations that advocate for workers' rights, and laws like the minimum wage are mechanisms that regulate the exploitation of workers. Unfortunately, it's not accurate to say that unions prevent the exploitation of workers, because if they are functioning within a capitalist system, workers are being exploited. While we should recognize the important role that unions play regarding workers' rights, we must also be honest about the context of exploitation they exist within.

It is important to get smarter about capitalism by remembering that while there is "no ethical consumption under capitalism," actively participating in the hoarding of resources and exploitation of workers is not the only way to operate within a capitalist system. There are three primary structures for capitalistic companies: for profit (ownership by shareholders), state-owned enterprises (ownership by the government), and worker cooperatives (ownership by workers). Not every company operates by exploitation, but determining whether or not it does often requires a thorough examination of its global supply chain, financial reports, and sustainability reports. The Spanish company Mondragon is the world's largest corporation based on the model of interconnected worker cooperatives (also called co-ops). It is worker owned and directed, and wages are determined though democratized voting, which has been successfully utilized since the company's founding in 1956. Workers should be the ones to benefit most from their labor, and while the Mondragon Corporation is still a retail service company that participates in capitalism, it does so in an innovative manner informed by socialism.

Ujamaa, an African socialist ideology implemented during political theorist and Pan-Africanist Julius Nyerere's presidency in Tanzania following the country's independence from Britain in 1961, is an excellent example of subverting the power structures and exploitation of capitalism. *Ujamaa* is a Swahili word meaning "community" or "togetherness" and in the context of Nyerere's policies, it can be understood as "cooperative economics."

The principles of ujamaa encompass elements of ubuntu through its emphasis on mutual respect and the inherent humanity and interconnectedness of all human beings. It recognizes that we cannot honor the interconnectedness of our humanity without simultaneously being cooperative in the sharing of resources. We can practice ujamaa by equitably compensating people for their labor according to their contributions. Instead of exploiting workers and paying people nothing at all or the bare minimum, ujamaa recognizes the need for economic justice that benefits communal goals over individuals aims.

Cooperative economics isn't exclusive to compensating people; it also includes the understanding that resources we do not need should be redistributed to those who do need them by virtue of their humanity and our collective interconnectedness. The impact of billionaires (who would fundamentally not be able to exist within a cooperative economics model) is best illustrated by this example: if all the billionaires in the United States used their income from March 2020 through January 2021 for the benefit of all the US people, they would easily be able to give $3,900 to every adult and child in the US and still remain the wealthiest people in the country. Just 651 people could provide immeasurable help to the estimated 331 million people in the United States and experience no adverse consequences.

"Living paycheck to paycheck," and "falling on hard times" are commonly used euphemisms that hide the fact that exploitation and impoverishment are the price that capitalist society has decided to pay in order to have billionaires. In 2020, while unemployment was at an all-time high, 56 people became billionaires. If wealth was redistributed as in the example above, not only would the economy improve, but more importantly, people's livelihoods would immediately improve, and the billionaires would face no adverse consequences. Wealth redistribution on this scale is incredibly unlikely to happen, however, because the super-rich have no incentive to provide direct aid to their fellow citizens except in the form of philanthropy and charity (in the United States charitable donations made to properly registered organizations can be used as tax write-offs). Instead of adequately taxing billionaires, our institutions promote the notion of philanthropy and charity to remedy the failures that result in this wealth chasm. But charity and philanthropy alone cannot offset the cost of impoverishment created by wealth hoarding. Economists agree that a good way to attempt to redistribute hoarded wealth is through higher federal and state taxes on the richest people in society. The current tax structure reveals that in many cases wealth-hoarding billionaires and corporations legally pay *nothing* in taxes. According to the Institute of Taxation and Economic Policy in 2020, a multiyear study of profitable US corporations showed that many paid zero taxes. For example, Delta Airlines and Chevron had a relative tax rate of –4 percent because of all the corporate tax rebates they were able to use. Yet addressing the policies that allow corporations and billionaires to evade accountability in the form of taxation wouldn't be enough; we also need to redress the global capitalism framework, potentially in the form of a global minimum tax rate. US Treasury Secretary Janet Yellen has advocated for a global minimum corporate tax rate to be established on an international level. Such tax structure would set a minimum tax rate on the profits of any qualifying multinational corporation. This would help to diminish the likelihood of corporations using countries with lower tax rates to shelter their income and avoid paying their fair share of taxes in countries with more comprehensive tax laws.

REFLECTION QUESTIONS

- How would you introduce yourself without talking about your work or area of study?
- How did learning about capitalism make you feel? Socialism? Did you learn anything new?
- What do you define as "labor"?
- What personal biases do you have about different occupations? Do you respect certain occupations more than others? Why is that? Where do you think you learned this?
- How is your labor classified? As unskilled, semiskilled, skilled, or professional? Do you agree with this classification?

CHAPTER 4

GET SMARTER ABOUT DISABILITY

Disability is an important part of humanity—there is no default way that humans move, understand, communicate, process, or exist. Following the guidance of the many disability scholars cited throughout this chapter, I use the terms *disabled* and *disability* in this book, though there is no single consensus on how to discuss or define disability. Disabled people are not a monolith, and there is great diversity in how disability is discussed within and outside the disability community. To get smarter about disability, we will emphasize approaches from intersectional disability theorists and scholars who are themselves disabled. In *Demystifying Disability* by Emily Ladau, disability and critical race scholar Imani Barbarin defines disability as "a holistic experience, so it must have a holistic definition. Disability is not just a physical diagnosis, but a lived experience in which parameters and barriers are placed upon our lives because of that diagnosis." Activist and speaker Rebecca Cokley defines disability as "a lens that crosses all communities and centers on the health implications and infinite creativity of a people subjected to ableism." *Ableism* is structural and interpersonal discrimination against people with disabilities. When defined in this manner, disability can be understood not only as a relationship to the conditions of ableist oppression, but also as a lived experience that involves surviving within that oppressive system. In institutions like the government of the United States, the definition of disability is far less descriptive. Therefore, it is important that these institutional definitions don't eclipse the ways disabled people self-define. According to the Centers for Disease Control and Prevention (CDC), a disability "is any condition of the body or mind (impairment) that makes it more difficult for the person with the condition to do certain activities (activity limitation) and interact with the world around them (participation restrictions)." The CDC's definition of disability fails to account for the ways that disabled people are restricted not by their disabilities, but by an ableist society that is not designed to accommodate the reality of all people—instead, ableist society only accommodates abled people.

Getting smarter about disability and accessibility requires us to understand that abled people are already accommodated within the oppressive structure that is ableism. Abled people are people who move, communicate, process, and exist in ways that society views as acceptable or even as the default. Abled people are not more worthy of respect, life, or humanity than disabled people, but ableism attempts to dictate otherwise. For example, ableist societies build stairs in places where ramps would serve the same utility because ableist negligence fails to account for the fact that stairs can only be used by some people. Ramps, on the other hand, allow for people of various mobility methods to access areas that are on an incline or decline. People who walk can use a ramp, and people who use wheelchairs, crutches, or motorized vehicles can also use a ramp. Not being able to use stairs is not a failure of disabled people—the ubiquity of stairs is a failure of an ableist society. Another example of this is the way people with speaking disabilities are marginalized by our society, which prioritizes spoken communication. Speaking is not the only or best way to communicate, but ableism determines that people who have speaking disabilities are "impaired" instead of simply understanding that there are countless ways humans communicate other than speech. The term *dumb* comes from the Dutch and German words meaning "stupid," and was once used to reference people who have speaking disabilities. While this usage is now considered archaic, the word is still used in a derogatory manner to insult someone's intelligence, a harmful legacy of ableist language. Intelligence, or the ability to acquire and apply knowledge and skills, cannot be measured against the rubric of ableism. As we get smarter about disability, we will examine how ableism perpetually dehumanizes disabled people, as well as how we can identify and fight ableism.

MODELS OF DISABILITY

There are three primary understandings, also called models, for learning about and addressing disability: the *medical model*, the *individual model*, and the *social model*. To get smarter about disability and ableism, we will start with an overview of each model, and then explore the critiques against them to contextualize and evaluate our understanding of disability and ableism.

As its name indicates, the *medical model* of disability emphasizes the role of the medical field in understanding disability. The medical model primarily understands disability as something to diagnose and treat, or "cure." Diagnosis (the process of identifying the symptoms of an illness, disability, or condition) and treatment can be helpful in accommodating and alleviating the challenges that come with some disabilities. For example, when I was eight years old, I took the Test of Variables of Attention (TOVA) to determine that I had attention deficit hyperactivity disorder (ADHD). With this medical diagnosis I was able to receive accommodations and treatment through therapy and medication. Unfortunately, there are many barriers to proper assessment, diagnosis, and treatment, such as income, availability, racism, sexism, and ableism. Gatekeeping access to the disabled community based on whether or not someone has a medical diagnosis is deeply classist and problematic, because access to medical care can be expensive and challenging. When diagnoses and/or treatments are available, the medical model of disability can be very helpful as a path forward. The medical model is not without its faults, however. Keah Brown, disabled scholar, actor, and author of *The Pretty One*, summarizes the medical model this way: "Within the medical model of disability is the inherent idea that disabled people need fixing or that we are broken. We are not broken." The implication that disabled people need to be "cured" or "fixed" is dangerous and dehumanizing.

Eugenics is the violent ideology that there are "good genes" and "bad genes" within the human species, and "bad genes" should be eradicated. The removal of "bad genes" is done through forced or coerced sterilization or other methods of preventing disabled people from reproducing. Positive eugenics advances the idea that people with "good genes" should reproduce, while negative eugenics advocates for the sterilization of people with "bad genes," but all eugenicist ideology is unscientific, supremacist, and harmful. Eugenicist ideology is unfortunately still prevalent, and has been used historically to harm disabled, racialized, LGBTQ+, Jewish, and Roma people. When medicine (or anything else) is used to target, dehumanize, harm, or eradicate communities, it must be denounced. In cases where the medical model of disability accounts for the historical and current nature of systems of oppression, it can be a worthwhile and helpful method of understanding disability. Technological advancements such as prosthetics, cochlear implants, and tests like the one I took to learn I have ADHD are all examples of appropriate and helpful uses of the medical model of disability.

The *individual model* of disability places the responsibility on disabled individuals to deal with the challenges that can come with having a disability. This understanding can positively emphasize the autonomy and agency of disabled people, who are often infantilized well into adulthood. The individual model is not entirely positive, however. In the United States, individualism is a core part of the national identity, and the notion of "pulling yourself up by your bootstraps" suggests that individuals alone can "overcome" hardship through discipline, sacrifice, and charisma. Tools like positive self-talk and discipline are generally good techniques to learn, but using these tools alone cannot free us from realities like ableist oppression. The individual model is often used to measure disabled people against each other. A disabled person who has low support needs at school and has access to health care, for example, may be presented as "proof" that other disabled people (who may have less access and/or greater support needs) can "make it" if they try hard enough. Disabled public figure and theoretical physicist Stephen Hawking is often used in support of this narrative. But pitting one or several disabled community members against the rest of the disability community is oppressive, and should be unlearned and avoided. The individual model of disability is problematic because it ignores that we all exist within the context of larger institutions and systems of oppression.

The *social model* of disability holds that disabled people are not impaired by their bodies or by medical diagnoses, but by ableist ideologies and social and literal constructions within society. This model, unlike the other two, was originated by disabled scholars. Rather than espousing the ableist perspective that disabled people simply "do not fit" in society, the social model clarifies the fact that it is actually our ableist society that creates and maintains a world full of obstacles that isolate disabled people. Societal systems and structures are constructed—both literally and figuratively—to accommodate abled people (who are included and provided access) while excluding disabled people (who are excluded and denied access). For example, if there is no wheelchair-accessible entrance to a location, the medical or individual models of disability incorrectly identify the individual using the wheelchair as the problem, while the social model understands that the problem is the location's lack of a ramp, elevator, or other wheelchair-accessible entrance. Placing the responsibility on individual people to resolve the structures in society that exclude them is oppressive, and when this is done to disabled people it is ableist. In terms of cognitive disabilities, ableism blames students with ADHD, for example, for being unable to sit still in class or focus for prolonged periods (a critique I heard often as a child), while an anti-ableist approach (informed by the social model) understands that the issue is actually the fact that schools are primarily designed to benefit those who can focus or sit still for prolonged periods of time (in ways deemed socially accepted or neurotypical). As disabled and neurodiverse people shift these understandings through scholarship, advocacy, and policy, institutions such as schools will need to accommodate students regardless of how they learn or demonstrate that learning. While legal protections like the Americans with Disabilities Act mandate that such accommodations be made, we cannot go from a deeply ableist society to an anti-ableist one through laws and policies alone. We have to get smarter about how we understand disability, and recognize that the humanity and worth of disabled people is inherent, not earned.

Even as we broaden our understanding of disability to center the lived experiences and realities of disabled people, we must be conscious to not participate in other forms of oppression simultaneously. Intersectionality, or the framework articulated by Dr. Kimberlé Crenshaw, emphasizes that people have multiple overlapping identities, and those identities are simultaneously impacted by oppressive structures. Intersectionality must be applied to any understanding of disability. For example, this would mean not participating in white supremacy by only focusing on *white* disabled people. Disability activist Vilissa Thompson created the hashtag #DisabilityTooWhite to name and create awareness of the fact that racialized disabled people are erased because ableism occurs in tandem with other systems of oppression like racism. Racialized disabled people are erased in depictions, scholarship, research, and evaluation tools relating to disability. One consequence of this is that racialized people are misdiagnosed and underdiagnosed at rates that can't be fully known due to the massive gaps in research and access. A 2009 study published in the *American Journal of Public Health* found that "significant racial/ethnic disparities exist in the recognition of Autism Spectrum Disorder." This perpetuates the racist notion that racialized people have a different physiology than white people, while in actuality all peoples have similar rates of disability. Such racialized erasure is a result of Eurocolonialism, which we will learn more about in the next chapter.

Other ableist understandings of disability include the *economic model* of disability, which looks at how much money someone can earn, how much work they can do, or how productive they are. This is classist, because it attempts to equate human value with economic productivity. Describing people as "high functioning" or "low functioning" is another problematic aspect of the economic model of disability. Functionality and productivity are relative terms, and no human needs to be or is productive all the time. What constitutes productivity is different for different people, and more importantly, our value as human beings is not defined by our work, our money, or our productivity. Everyone inherently deserves respect, no matter what or if they produce.

Finally, the *tragedy model* of disability treats disability as something that is tragic, or inherently involves loss. The tragedy model often prioritizes people who have become disabled over the course of their lives and deprioritizes people born with disabilities, which is fundamentally ableist. Getting smarter about ableism means unlearning the impulse to make assumptions about other people's lives. No one is entitled to know the diagnosis, prognosis, or origin of a person's disability. Through the tragedy model, disabled people are treated as objects of pity, not out of genuine empathy, but often from a place of internalized ableism. In this context, disabled people are hailed as inspirational for "overcoming" their disability. As Imani Barbarin says, "I do not overcome my disability, I overcome ableist assumptions." Whether or not we have intentionally internalized ableism, it is our responsibility to do better and to unlearn these biases and oppressive attitudes once we know better. Disability is not something synonymous with death, loss, or despair—it is a multifaceted experience that cannot and should not be reduced to a singular one.

TALKING ABOUT DISABILITY

There is no one right way to talk about disability. The use of language varies greatly within the disabled community and can depend on current, historical, personal, and circumstantial contexts. That said, there are some general do's and don'ts when it comes to describing disabilities and disabled people. The most important thing to know is that disabled people are entitled to make their own decisions about how they self-identify and self-describe. It's crucial to respect and affirm the ways that people describe themselves, even if they may differ from how you choose to describe yourself or your disability.

There are two main ways of referring to disability: *person-first language* (PFL) and *identity-first language* (IFL). Neither of these options are inherently wrong. As with the many ways of describing ourselves and others, usage may differ between and across different communities. (In this book, I alternate between PFL and IFL depending on the context and what is most respectful.) Person-first language literally centers the person before the disability, as in a "person with a disability" or a "person with asthma." Advocates of PFL seek to emphasize the personhood or humanity of a disabled person before their disability status. On the other hand, many people consider disability to be an intimate part of what constitutes their personal identity, so they do not feel that the intention of PFL is necessary because disability does not negate or take away from their personhood or humanity—ableism does. Getting smarter about disability means reflecting on whether our inclination toward PFL or IFL is based on respecting other people or alleviating our ableist biases. Identity-first language, on the other hand, positions disability as core to identity by putting it first, as in "disabled person" or "autistic person." Advocates of IFL often choose it because it centers their disabled identity and connects them to the larger disability community and culture. However, depending on the disability you are describing, IFL might not always be appropriate or make sense—for example, you shouldn't call someone a "Down syndrome person" or a "dwarfism person." Instead, in these examples, a "person with Down syndrome" or "person with dwarfism" is the correct and respectful way to discuss these disabilities.

Part of fighting ableism is recognizing that disabled people are not a monolith and that there is no uniform approach to the language used to describe disability. This is totally okay. When possible and appropriate, be sure to ask the person you are describing what terminology is respectful to them ("How do you describe yourself?"). If you are disabled, sharing with and informing people of what you are partial to ("I use identity-first language, so you can say I'm a 'disabled person'") and correcting people accordingly is appropriate and helpful, but it depends on your own comfort level. If you're ever unsure about the specific and correct terminology to use when referencing a community, ask yourself why you're in a position to describe that community without being connected or in conversation with them. Further, make sure that you're not relying on previously held understandings of what language might be appropriate. Take the time to do research, seek out community-created or collaborative resources, and find organizations led by and centering the community and see which language they're using. To determine if an organization is a trustworthy source, be sure to identify whether the organization is reflective of a given community by looking at their leadership, funding, and reception within the community.

Beyond PFL and IFL, there are other considerations when talking about disability. Euphemisms for disability, such as "special needs," "differently abled," "challenged," "handicapped," and "handicapable," are all terms that were developed by nondisabled people and should generally be avoided. According to Rebecca Cokley, using euphemisms instead of accurate and specific language perpetuates ableism. For example, the phrase "special needs" is not legally defined or enforceable within legislation like the Americans with Disabilities Act, and its application can be infantilizing when used in reference to adults, since the language of "needs" is usually applied to children. This phrase also focuses language around services and accommodations instead of around the people and community themselves. Not only does this create an ableist hierarchy of those with "basic needs" and those with "special needs," but it also glosses over the fact that *everyone* has needs. In reality, rather than benefiting from "special treatment," disabled people are more often forced to navigate and survive within a world that refuses to honor their humanity or even consider their needs at all. So rather than saying "special needs," say "accommodations" because we all require specific accommodations to survive and thrive within various contexts. (Note that if someone prefers the term "special needs" to describe themselves, that should be respected and not dismissed.) "Handicapped" is another term that is generally considered to be disrespectful within the disability community (the word actually originates from sports and horse betting and should never be used to describe people). Rather than using this term to describe things like entrances, parking spots, or bathroom stalls, the best word to use is "accessible." Similarly, it's inappropriate to describe someone as "high functioning" or "low functioning," and it's *never* okay for abled people to use ableist slurs.

TYPES OF DISABILITY

To provide the best possible overview of the different types of disabilities, I worked with disabled scholars Keah Brown, Imani Barbarin, and Rebecca Cokley to explore disability across the categories of mobility, hearing, seeing, communication, developmental, cognitive, chronic illness, neurological, psychiatric, and substance use or addiction. These categories are not exhaustive, nor are they mutually exclusive. Someone may have both a hearing disability and a mobility disability, and the two may or may not be connected. There is no one way to be disabled or have a disability, so we should not expect to be able to conclusively define and measure all disabled people. This is okay. The only person who gets to define a person's disability is that person.

Not all disabilities are noticeable or externally apparent—for example, you may not be able to tell if someone experiences chronic pain or has a psychiatric disability—but they are still disabilities, and it's generally not our business to determine either way. It is not up to others to fulfill our assumptions or curiosities; rather, it is up to us to disrupt and examine our assumptions and educate ourselves. Some of the subjects described on the following pages may not always be discussed under the umbrella of "disability," but they are considered disabilities within emerging understandings and/or by many of the people who experience them. Furthermore, just because someone has some of the characteristics associated with a given disability doesn't necessarily mean that they self-identify as disabled, and that is okay.

DISABILITY TERMINOLOGY

NAME	DESCRIPTION	ADDITIONAL INFORMATION
Autism or autism spectrum disorder	Autism is a type of *neurodiversity*, or difference in cognitive, neurological, or developmental processes that can be understood as different ways of communicating, understanding, being, thinking, and socializing. There is no one way of being autistic.	Autism should not be understood in a binary of "high functioning" and "low functioning." Instead, the terms "high support needs" and "low support needs" should be used to describe someone's support needs in various contexts.
Chronic illness	Chronic illness is not itself always defined as a disability, but it may involve factors that are disabling to physical or mental health. A chronic illness is any illness that lasts more than three months or more than a year depending on definitions.	Someone may have a chronic illness and also be healthy. Health is not the absence of illness. Euphemisms like "underlying condition" and "preexisting condition" are often used to describe chronic illness, but these are not always accurate and carry a stigma.
Cognitive disability	Disabilities related to or involving the cognitive functions of processing, recalling, communicating, and applying information. This may include diagnoses like ADHD, dyslexia (difficulty with reading), and dyscalculia (difficulty with numbers).	The terms "intellectual disability" and "learning disability" are being phased out because they imply that an individual's intelligence (or ability to acquire and apply knowledge and skills) should be defined by the limited ways that society measures cognitive functions.

DISABILITY TERMINOLOGY

NAME	DESCRIPTION	ADDITIONAL INFORMATION
Developmental disability	Disabilities related to an individual's development. This category of disability is extremely broad and can relate to any mental and/or physical development.	There is no single "normal" way that humans develop, but ableist society is designed to only accommodate nondisabled people.
Hearing disability	Disabilities related to hearing or the perception of information with the ears. People with hearing disabilities may be described as deaf or hard of hearing. They may use assistive devices, such as hearing aids or cochlear implants, and some may use sign language and/or lip read. (It should not, however, be assumed that all people with hearing disabilities use sign language.)	People who do not have hearing disabilities are known as "hearing people." Always use a microphone when speaking to a large group, and do not assume that everyone is hearing. Tools such as captioning and sign language interpretation are also assistive and should be offered. Discrimination against people with hearing disabilities is called *audism*.
Mobility disability	Disabilities related to movement or mobility. People with mobility disabilities may use assistive devices, such as wheelchairs, walkers, or crutches.	Use terminology like "wheelchair user" instead of "wheelchair bound." Remember that there are also ambulatory wheelchair users, or people who use wheelchairs and can walk.
Neurological disability	Disabilities related to the nerves and nervous system, like the brain and spine. Neurological disabilities may include epilepsy, multiple sclerosis, and Parkinson's disease.	Neurological disabilities can be congenital or acquired. It is important to not make assumptions about whether an individual's neurological disability is either of these.

CONTINUED

DISABILITY TERMINOLOGY

NAME	DESCRIPTION	ADDITIONAL INFORMATION
Psychiatric disability	Disabilities related to mental health, including but not limited to perception, mood, and behavior. They may result from life events, traumatic events, and/or environmental factors, or may be the result of naturally occurring chemical imbalances. Examples include bipolar disorder, anxiety, and depression.	Psychiatric disability is sometimes described as "mental illness." This is a misnomer because illness implies a sickness to be cured instead of the reality that human brain chemistry is varied and should be accommodated. Avoid using psychiatric disabilities in a flippant manner to describe emotional states like, "I'm so OCD." This is demeaning and contributes to stigma.
Seeing disability	Disabilities related to vision or perception of information with the eyes. People with seeing disabilities are often described as blind, legally blind, or as having low vision, and seeing disabilities are a spectrum, not a binary. People who are legally recognized as blind may be able to see shapes, light, and colors.	Tools to accommodate seeing disabilities include glasses, support animals, braille, and descriptive language to contextualize visual information.
Substance use disorders/addiction	Disability that can be related to many different factors, but involves the disordered use of a substance like food, alcohol, or chemicals. Because of harmful social, legal, cultural, religious, and moral connotations and stigma, addiction is rarely recognized as a condition or disability, but research conclusively demonstrates that it should be.	Addiction is not a character flaw or a failure of willpower. Substance use disorder can be connected to psychiatric disabilities, but not always. It is important not to place value judgments on which addictions are considered more "acceptable," because this creates ableist barriers.

ABLEISM

Ableism is the systematic prioritization of abled people over disabled people and the resulting marginalization of disabled people. It is a type of supremacism (an incorrect belief that certain people are superior to others) that treats disabled people (or those who are perceived to be disabled) as inferior to those who are (or are perceived to be) abled. Ableism also describes the internalized beliefs held about disabled people by abled and disabled people alike, as well as the internalized beliefs we hold toward ourselves. Ableism teaches abled people to base their sense of self on their abled status, which is inherently temporary. This system of oppression is reinforced through the media, policy, and interpersonal and institutional contexts. Abled people often participate in ableism by expressing pity for disabled people, not due to genuine empathy for the ableism someone may be enduring, but out of fear that they may themselves become disabled and experience ableism. Instead of viewing disability as a societal problem (which is ableist), we would all be better served by understanding ableism as the issue in need of redress.

When disability is defined in terms of productivity or level of "functioning," the emphasis is placed on what a disabled person "contributes" to society or the economy. But people do not need to be productive or "high functioning" in order to be worthy of respect and dignity. These things are inherent to our humanity. Ableism defines disabled people as less worthy because they are seen to "contribute less," while it simultaneously restricts the ways that disabled people are able to participate in society. In 2020, according to the United States Bureau of Labor Statistics, "across all age groups persons with disabilities were much less likely to be employed than those with no disabilities," and the same was true "across all educational attainment groups." The opportunities made available to disabled people are reflections of ableism, not the limitations of disabled people.

Ableism is so pervasive in Eurocolonial societies that it is even woven into our language, with many ableist terms, sayings, and phrases in constant popular use. For example, terms like "crazy" have long been used to stigmatize people with psychiatric disabilities, while words like "moron" and "idiot" were historically used as pseudoscientific medical diagnoses of people with cognitive and developmental disabilities. Similarly, disabilities are often appropriated in a negative context in figures of speech, such as "blind to" or "fell on deaf ears." Most people don't think about this when they use such terms in casual conversation, but the fact that these words and phrases are ableist must be recognized and their use must be discontinued, because ableist language contributes to stigma and harm. As you examine and challenge the ableist language that you may use, keep in mind that there are many other ways to describe things that do not require being harmful to other people. We may use this language without being aware that it is harmful, but once we know better, it is our responsibility to do better.

ABLEIST LANGUAGE

WHAT NOT TO SAY	WHAT TO SAY INSTEAD	WHY
"suffers from," "afflicted by"	"a person with," "a person who has"	It's rude and inappropriate to qualify disability with stigmatizing language.
"moron," "idiot," "stupid," "dumb," "imbecile," R-word	Nothing; don't insult people based on their actual or perceived intelligence or common sense.	There is a painful history of terms like these being used to diagnose people with cognitive and developmental disabilities.
"color-blind racism"	"racist negligence"	People who do not perceive specific colors still experience and participate in racism. Avoid ableism by being specific about what is meant when someone claims to "not see color."
"crazy," "lunatic," "insane," "psycho"	"passionate," "bizarre," "erratic"	These terms have been used to stigmatize psychiatric disabilities, and using these terms contributes to the current stigma.
"tone deaf"	"disrespectful," "inappropriate," "in poor taste"	Rather than framing deafness in a negative context, discuss what may or may not be appropriate without making it about disability.
"turn a blind eye," "blind to," "fall on deaf ears"	"ignore," "disregard"	Blind and deaf people are not intentionally blind or deaf. Do not use disability in euphemisms that make it seem so.

REFLECTION QUESTIONS

- How has ableism impacted your life? What examples of ableism do you see in the media?

- Do you ever use the ableist language listed on page 93? If so, how will you work on this?

- Everyone benefits from accessibility, whether you're disabled or not. What are some examples of the tools or accommodations that you use in your life?

- Where did you first learn about disability? Has this changed throughout your life? How and why?

- Which models of understanding disability resonate with you? Why?

CHAPTER 5

GET SMARTER ABOUT RACE AND RACISM

As a Black person, I have often been asked, "Why do you have to bring race into this?" This question usually makes me laugh, because I deal with frustration through humor, but it also makes me reflect on the reality that race is a massive part of my life as a Black person in the United States. I do not bring race into things; I was brought into race. Human beings have existed for 200,000 years, but "race" has existed for only about 600 years. Race is not a biological fact, or even something that humans discovered and *then* exploited to oppress others. Race was *invented* and *implemented* specifically for the purposes of oppression. In this chapter we will learn about the invention and implementation of race and the ensuing consequences.

Political and race theorist Dr. Utz McKnight explains that race is not what describes human difference, but what humans use to create the possibility of difference. Racism uses race to create difference and then assigns meaning to and ranks humans as superior or inferior based on those differences. As explained by Dr. Dorothy Roberts, acclaimed scholar of race, gender, and the law, "Race is not a biological category that is politically charged. It is a political category that has been disguised as a biological one." Race is not a fact of biology or genetics, but because of its impact on all elements of society, it is a very real aspect of life that we must examine and get smarter about.

Race and racism permeate every corner of society that has been touched by European colonization. In this chapter we will explore how it is internalized by us (intrapersonal racism), affects our interactions (interpersonal racism), and impacts the larger infrastructures that control society (institutional racism). In the United States, for example, race and racism exist to serve and maintain white supremacy. As we get smarter about race and racism, we must be prepared to do lots of unlearning and relearning.

RACE

Race is an active hierarchical division of human beings that serves to create and perpetuate racialized and racist social structures. *Hierarchical* means divided into different ranked or tiered levels that are assigned unequal value. *Racialization* is the categorization or division of people according to race. Throughout this book I use the phrase "racialized people" to describe all people who are categorized according to race. Importantly, I specifically name whiteness because "white" is an often unspoken position of power created by racialization and must be identified accordingly. (We'll get smarter about that issue in this chapter as well.)

Racism is a Eurocolonial system that dictates how we should exist, behave, interact, regulate, and organize ourselves and each other. Widely accepted definitions of race, like those found in a dictionary, often incorrectly describe race as "the major groupings into which humankind is divided on the basis of physical characteristics or shared ancestry." This definition is false, and the assertion that race is based on physical characteristics or shared ancestry is a racist lie. In 2019, the American Association of Physical Anthropologists stated, "Race does not provide an accurate representation of human biological variation." That is to say that while human biological variations or differences like our facial features, hair textures, skin colors, and more do exist, these differences are not what constitute race. Scientific research has conclusively determined that "race" is not genetic or biological, nor is it a naturally occurring phenomenon. Race is a human invention, and to get smarter about it we must define it in the context of the power dynamics it creates.

Another way of saying that race is a human invention is to say that it is a *social construct*. Social constructions are the ways humans organize society to support their assumptions about humanity. In terms of race, these assumptions include two key elements described by historian and anthropologist Patrick Wolfe: (1) "difference is not neutral: to vary is to be defective" and (2) race "links physical characteristics to cognitive, cultural, and moral ones." These assumptions are not based on evidence or reality. Instead, the ways we define reality have been constructed to reinforce racist lies. How humans perpetuate, maintain, and recreate social constructs over time is called *social reproduction*. Many things that are widely accepted as facts in society are reproduced constructs. For example, the calendar is a construct. In most of the world, time is measured by the Gregorian calendar, which splits the year into 365 days, twelve months, and a seven-day week. While it may seem that this is the only way to divide time and the way it's been done forever, this calendar has actually only been in use since 1582. Before the Gregorian calendar, different societies used different measurements of time, but as trade increased and colonization emerged, the need for a standardized system of time measurement became necessary. This calendar has been socially reproduced on increasingly large scales since its establishment. Because the Catholic church is a major religious, political, and economic institution, Pope Gregory XIII (for whom the calendar is named) was able to issue a papal bull (or official decree) as a means of establishing this construct.

Unlike the Gregorian calendar, which helps us measure the passage of time, the construct of race was created to categorize people and justify the dehumanization necessary for European colonization. According to biological anthropologist, sociologist, evolutionary geneticist, and critical race scholar Dr. Shay-Akil McLean, "Race/ism was created by European colonizers in order to seize land, labor, and gain control of the means of production." Following the decline of European feudalism in the fourteenth century, Europe's economy shifted from being based on land and labor to being based on trade and the exchange of capital. Unable to survive solely on the conquest of land and people in Europe, countries such as Portugal, France, Belgium, Spain, and Britain looked outward to what would become known as Africa and the "New World" (the Americas) in search of land to colonize and resources to exploit, such as human beings, animals, gold, spices, and sugar.

Portuguese monarchs ordered the invasion of North Africa for the purposes of capturing land and people as early as 1415. Historians estimate that some of the first enslaved Africans may have been people from Mauritania captured during raids by the Portuguese. While these invasions were already occurring, they had not yet been granted legitimacy and approval from the Pope. So, in 1452, a papal bull called *Dum Diversas,* which translates to "until different," was issued by Pope Nicholas V. This authorized the perpetual enslavement and removal of the "enemies of Christ, wheresoever placed," which provided all Catholic invaders with a "divine" basis for the enslavement and dehumanization of Indigenous peoples in Africa and the Americas in addition to the Muslim, Jewish, and other non-Christian peoples who were already facing persecution through Christian crusades and inquisitions.

The people in the lands that these colonizers invaded were racialized (or categorized according to the construct of race) to falsely classify

African and other Indigenous peoples as "subhuman" and in need of the intervention and domination of colonialism. With every new imperialist mission, the colonizers racialized the Indigenous peoples and placed them into the hierarchy created by race. *Indigenous* means "originating or occurring naturally in a particular place." It is also a synonym for native (though depending on context, these terms may not be interchangeable). Any people who are indigenous to a region are Indigenous peoples; however, this terminology is often exclusively applied to people within the Americas and Australia, even though African peoples are also Indigenous peoples. It's important to note that indigeneity is a relative position within a colonial system, so it is inaccurate to refer to the colonizing peoples of Europe as Indigenous peoples as this terminology and understanding was not created until Europeans invaded other lands.

As explained by journalist and political scholar Claudia Jones, *imperialism* (or expanding a country's power and influence through colonization) is "the root cause of racialism. It is the ideology which upholds colonial rule and exploitation. It preaches the "superiority" of the white race whose "destiny" it is to rule over those with colored skins, and to treat them with contempt." While colonization may feel like it happened long ago, colonialism is ongoing and its ideology continues as "white paternalism" (also called "white saviorism" or archaically "white man's burden"), which is the oppressive idea that white people have a "duty" to intervene in the lives of all racialized people in order for us to thrive or otherwise be successful. White paternalism is the ideology that underpins practices like overpolicing in predominantly Black neighborhoods, for example.

Throughout the early era of European colonization, the construct of race was a convenient tool and shorthand for categorizing (or racializing) humans in order to oppress them. Since that period, racist legal and pseudoscientific systems have adapted and evolved to define race more narrowly, with the effects still felt to this day.

The following is a brief annotated historical timeline of the invention and reproduction of race from 1452 to 1950.

1452: The papal bull *Dum Diversas* from Pope Nicholas V on the "enemies of Christ" is used to subjugate and enslave Indigenous peoples in Africa and the Americas, and to continue the ongoing campaigns of violence and discrimination against Jewish, Muslim, and other non-Christian peoples.

1492: The Spanish Edict of Expulsion forcibly displaces 200,000 Jewish people from Spain and Portugal as part of the Spanish Inquisition. Simultaneously, Spain funds Christopher Columbus's invasion of the Americas and attempted genocide of the Indigenous peoples of Turtle Island (what would come to be called North America).

1500: The Age of Enlightenment begins. Europeans begin using "science" and philosophy in addition to religion to reproduce race and racism. The idea of the Great Chain of Being is used to place Europeans closer to God in the racial hierarchy, with all racialized people below them.

1513–1604: Spain, Britain, and France continue to invade North America and establish colonies through displacement and violence. The first African people are enslaved and transported to British colonies.

1662: *Partus sequitur ventrum* (or "the offspring follows the belly") becomes law in the Virginia colony, which extends the status of enslavement and chattel slavery from mother to child, further codifying the human reproduction aspect in the process of the social reproduction of race.

1664: A law passed in the Maryland General Assembly uses two legal criteria, "a black skin and residency in Maryland," to interconnect the condition of enslavement with racialized Blackness. This codifies the belief that all Black people, enslaved or free, were designated as enslaved people. This also serves to provide a basis "for holding Black Christians in perpetual bondage."

1685: The Code Noir decree is issued by King Louis XIV to control free and enslaved Black people in the French territories of the Americas. The code requires the indoctrination of enslaved Black people into Christianity and limits the civil and citizenship rights of freed Black people. For example, people of European and racialized parentage could not use the last name of their European parent.

1691: "White" first appears in reference to white people in the Virginia colony for the purposes of banning marriage between Black and white people. This begins a long history of "anti-miscegenation" laws in the United States, which ban marriage or reproduction between racialized peoples and white people.

1749: French naturalist and scientific racist Georges-Louis Leclerc introduces race (and racism) to the "scientific" study of human variation.

1758: Swedish botanist and scientific racist Carl Linnaeus classifies human beings into six variations, with descriptions for skin color, body features, hair color, hair texture, eye color, behavior, form of government, and clothing. Even though Linnaeus does not use the term "race," the descriptions he attaches to the variations he invented are deeply and objectively racist. These six variations included wild people (*Homo sapiens ferus*), red people (*Homo sapiens Americanus*), white people (*Homo sapiens Europaeus*), yellow people (*Homo sapiens Asiaticus*), black people (*Homo sapiens Africanus*), and monster people (*Homo sapiens monstrosus*).

1787: German racist Christoph Meiners publishes *Outline of the Theory and History of the Beautiful Sciences*, which advances harmful ideologies like the "superior" beauty, intelligence, and brain size of Europeans over all racialized people, including Indigenous peoples in the Americas and Africa, Jewish peoples, and Slavic peoples. Meiners also claims that racialized people feel pain and emotion to a lesser degree than Europeans.

1792: Dutch physician and racist Petrus Camper codifies "featurism" in the form of facial angle measurement to categorize human facial features into a hierarchy that places Europeans at the top.

1795: German anatomist and racist Johann Blumenbach categorizes humans into five varieties, including "Caucasian," "Mongolian," "Malayan," "Negro," and "American." This is significant because it is the understanding of racism that most of the world still operates from, placing emphasis on color, features, and country of origin to determine who can and cannot participate in society and be considered deserving of humanity.

1799: Founding father, physician, and racist Benjamin Rush proposes the idea of "negroidism," a nonexistent medical condition that claims people with darker skin are actually white skinned and in need of treatment for a (nonexistent) form of leprosy, which had darkened their skin color. (Rush is primarily known for being one of the fifty-six people signed the United States Declaration of Independence.)

1839: Physicians and racists Samuel Morton and George Combe advance the pseudoscience of phrenology, which falsely claims that differences in skull size—and therefore intellectual capacity—are based on race.

1857: The yearlong Indian Rebellion of 1857 begins in an attempt to end the colonial rule of the British East India Company. Following the suppression of the uprising, power is transferred from the British East India Company to the British monarchy. Under this new rule, colonizers implement racialized policies against intermarriage between racialized people and white people and mandate the segregation of Indian people.

1865: Chattel slavery and involuntary servitude ends in the United States (except as punishment for a crime).

1870: The Naturalization Act allows for "aliens of African nativity" and "persons of African descent" to become United States citizens. The US Census includes racialized categories for "color," including "B" for Black, "C" for Chinese/East Asian, "I" for American Indian, "M" for Mulatto, and "W" for white.

1872: English biologist, naturalist, and racist Charles Darwin publishes *The Descent of Man, and Selection in Relation to Sex*, and claims that the human species consists of separate biological races, and that variations in skin tone, hair texture, facial features, and more are "evidence" of this. Darwin suggests that biological race has been created through either sexual selection or natural selection. He also asserts that when distinct biological races reproduce or "mix," they form new distinct races. This uses baseless pseudoscience to incite continued panic about racial "impurity" resulting from "miscegenation."

1877: Former New York state senator and racist Lewis Henry Morgan labels the stages of human progress as "savagery," "barbarism," and "civilization," placing European societies as the highest and most refined form of human progress. While Morgan did not invent this Enlightenment-era notion, he reproduces and perpetuates it.

1882: The United States implements the Chinese Exclusion Act, suspending immigration for and naturalization of people from China. In 1892, Congress extends this law, which is made permanent in 1902 and not formally repealed until 1943.

1890: The United States begins using eight primary classifications of race, relying on the assumptions advanced by Blumenbach and Darwin to create categories including white, Black (¾ or more "Black blood"), Mulatto (⅜ to ⅝ "Black blood"), Quadroon (¼ "Black blood"), Octoroon (⅛ "Black blood"), Indian, Chinese, and Japanese.

1896: The *Plessy v. Ferguson* decision is handed down, with the US Supreme Court holding that racial segregation laws for public facilities are constitutional so long as the segregated facilities are equal in quality, a doctrine that comes to be known as "separate but equal." (In practice this becomes "separate and superior" for white people.) This doctrine is inherently white supremacist as it separates racialized people from white people in all aspects of public life and death (with even cemeteries being segregated).

1898–1941: The US immigration and naturalization laws racialize Jewish people as part of the "Hebrew race."

1900: The US Census categories for color or race include "B" for Black, "Ch" for Chinese, "In" for American Indian, "Jp" for Japanese, and "W" for white. It also adds a separate "Indian Population Schedule" with a question regarding the "fraction of a person's lineage that is white."

1910: The US Census adds categories for color or race including "Ot" for "other" races. In the 1910 Indian Population Schedule, there are three separate questions about the proportion of a person's lineage that is American Indian, Black, and white.

1920: The Indian Population Schedule is removed from the US Census.

1924: The Immigration Act of 1924 is signed into law by President Calvin Coolidge with the declaration that "America must be kept American." The act sets a limit on the number of immigration visas to 2 percent of the total number of people of each nationality that were in the United States as of the 1890 national census. The legislation targets Asian, Polish, Italian, Greek, and Slavic immigrants, as well as Jewish immigrants (racialized as belonging to the "Hebrew race").

1925: The US Army War College issues a memorandum titled "The Use of Negro Manpower in War," which presents racist pseudoscience alleging that Black pilots cannot match the prowess of white pilots. This memorandum encourages the continued segregation of the US military.

1930: Racialized categories for the US Census include "Ch" for Chinese, "Fil" for Filipino, "Hin" for Hindu, "In" for American Indian, "Jp" for Japanese, "Kor" for Korean, "Mex" for Mexican, "Neg" for Black, and "W" for white. All other races are to be written out in full. According to the US Census history, "A person with both white and Black lineage was to be recorded as Black, no matter [the] fraction of that lineage. A person of mixed Black and American Indian lineage was also to be recorded as Black, unless he was considered to be 'predominantly' American Indian and accepted as such within the community." This erases the Black Americans and Americans of African descent who may have had Indigenous American ancestry without tribal membership or recognition.

1933–1945: Reprehensible laws are passed against Jewish peoples in Europe by the Nazi regime, including the Nuremberg Laws of 1935, which strip citizenship and civil rights from Jewish people on the basis of a racialized designation of "a Jewish race." By 1945 an estimated six million Jewish people will have been systematically murdered during the Holocaust. During this time period, the United States refuses entry to ships of Jewish refugees fleeing Nazi persecution.

1940: The United States creates the Alien Registration Act, which requires that all immigrants age fourteen and up register with the government and be fingerprinted as a matter of "national security." What constitutes "Americanness," loyalty, and patriotism excludes racialized people whether they are born in the United States or not. "Mexican" is removed as a racialized category, and people who had previously been recorded as Mexican are now recorded as white "unless definitely of Indian or other nonwhite ancestry."

1942–1945: Following the Imperial Japanese Army's attack on Pearl Harbor, the United States falsely justifies the incarceration of Japanese Americans and people of Japanese descent, claiming that people of Japanese ancestry posed an inherent national security risk using the false definitions of national loyalty and patriotism to racialized identity. Data recorded in the 1940 US Census is used to rob and incarcerate Japanese and Japanese American people.

1901–1949: Australia implements the White Australia policy, best (though harmfully) described by then prime minister John Curtin as follows: "This country shall remain forever the home of the descendants of those people who came here . . . in order to establish in the South Seas an outpost of the British race."

1949: South Africa's Prohibition of Mixed Marriages Act becomes law under apartheid, forbidding "miscegenation," or marriage between racialized people and white people.

1950: Race, not color, is used to record racialization on the US Census.

Examining the timeline, we can see the incremental changes and absurd ideas that laid the foundation for our current system of race and racism. A key point in this process was the shift from using religion to marginalize people to the Age of Enlightenment practice of using "science" and philosophy to articulate difference, and law to rank that difference and oppress people accordingly.

WHITENESS AND WHITE SUPREMACY

As race and racism were invented, implemented, and perpetuated, whiteness and white supremacy were simultaneously invented, implemented, and perpetuated. By constructing race and reproducing it as necessary, Europeans racialized all other human beings as secondary and lesser to themselves (or, more colloquially, as lesser to "white people"). Whiteness (or the condition of being white) is a position of power only made possible by the creation of racialized groups like Black people, Indigenous people, and people of color. "White" is also a racialized identity; however, in systems of white supremacy, there is no racism against white people. Feminist writer, speaker, activist, and social worker Michelle B. Taylor notes how even the phrase "people of color" implies that there are people without color, or white people, who are synonymous with the default state of being a human (who are simply "people"). Race, racism, and racialization dictate who is and is not human or deserving of humanity. The way racialization impacts white people is by leaving them unnamed as white and unimpacted by the consequences of race and racism. Children with one racialized parent and one white parent are often described as "half-Black," "half-Indian," etc., while it is assumed that the other unnamed "half" is white. This is also demonstrated in the way that racialized people are often forced to hyphenate our racialized identity with our national identity, such as Asian-American, African-American, and so on. Without these hyphenations the default assumption is whiteness. It was best said by Nobel Prize–winning author Toni Morrison, "In this country American means white. Everybody else has to hyphenate." For this reason it is important to disrupt the power dynamic of whiteness by naming it in circumstances where whiteness would otherwise go unspoken.

Through the invention of race and racism, European colonizers became "white people" and whiteness became the baseline of what it meant to be human. This self-definition was reproduced within the work of countless European Enlightenment-era philosophers, including but not limited to David Hume, René Descartes, Thomas Locke, and Immanuel Kant. These and other European philosophers explained what it meant to be a human being from their own self-benefiting position as white European men. As African diaspora and gender studies professor Dr. Sabine Broeck explains, "The human right to knowledge, self-possession and mastery" is "given as an exclusive birthright to white western Europeans by the Enlightenment scholars because of the self-declared 'beauty' of the Caucasian race." The very definition of "beauty" that is still perpetuated today comes from the eighteenth-century fabrications of Christoph Meiners, which are falsely presented as fact.

It is crucial to understand that whiteness is a position of power within the system of race—it is the default in any structure that is built upon white supremacy. The Eurocolonial assumptions about race as a system that we examined in the previous section are required in order for whiteness and white supremacy to continue to exist. If everyone were to get smarter about race, racism, whiteness, and white supremacy as they have been summarized here, then the entire foundation of this 600-year-old system of oppression would begin to collapse. Despite the suggestions of acclaimed scientists like Charles Darwin, Johann Blumenbach, and Carl Linnaeus, white supremacy is not based in the natural world, but in the fabricated and self-fulfilled prophesies they created and called "science." White supremacy is a system that falsely places whiteness and white people at the center of what it means to be human, to live, and to be deserving of humanity and livelihood. Yet white supremacy is not only maintained by race and racism; it's also upheld by antisemitism, which we must also get smarter about.

ANTISEMITISM

As we can see in the timeline on pages 100–106, another underpinning of white supremacy is antisemitism. In fact, antisemitism is older than race and racism, dating back to at least 270 BCE, with the earliest anti-Jewish writings recorded by historians. As the history of the Jewish people is ancient, complex, and cannot fit into a small section of a book, we will focus here on getting smarter about a few important introductory concepts with regard to antisemitism. It's important to keep in mind that discussing antisemitism exclusively as religious persecution may be harmful because it erases the reality of ethnic and racialized discrimination that has long been part of antisemitism. Similarly, discussing antisemitism exclusively in the context of racism may be perceived as harmful because the idea of a "Jewish race" is an archaic and inaccurate way to describe Jewish identity, though we should understand that antisemitism or anti-Jewish hatred is inherently racialized in the context of white supremacy.

Jewish identity may relate to religion, ethnicity, shared ancestry, shared history, religious and/or secular traditions, and culture. As noted in the previous timeline, throughout history Jewish people have experienced persecution, ostracization, and mass expulsions through anti-Jewish laws like the 1492 Edict of Expulsion, which forcibly displaced 200,000 Jewish people from Spain and Portugal as part of the Spanish Inquisition. According to Jewish educator Hilary Hawn, antisemitism "transcends political ideologies" and is "deeply ingrained in the collective psyche, so much so that it can often be hard to recognize. That's why it's so important to familiarize oneself with the way it looks and functions." The International Holocaust Remembrance Alliance (IHRA) defines antisemitism as "a certain perception of [Jewish people], which may be expressed as hatred toward [Jewish people]. Rhetorical and physical manifestations of antisemitism are directed toward Jewish or non-Jewish individuals and/ or their property, toward Jewish community institutions and religious facilities." As noted by the IHRA definition, antisemitism isn't always violence; it's also a dehumanized perception of Jewish people that stems from white supremacist institutions that propagate ignorance, intolerance, and fear, which ultimately leads to violence. Antisemitism also manifests as denying the reality and pervasiveness of antisemitism throughout history and in the present, and/or denying the reality and consequences of the Holocaust. The Holocaust describes the systematic displacement, persecution, and murder of over six million Jewish people by the Nazi regime during World War II. Antisemitism did not begin with or end following the Holocaust, and to claim otherwise is itself antisemitic.

Antisemitism is often demonstrated through the general dehumanization of, stigmatization of, violence toward, maligning of, and stereotyping of individual Jewish people and broader Jewish communities. A fixture of antisemitic hate speech includes what the IHRA describes as a "Jewish conspiracy" of Jewish people "controlling the media, economy, government or other societal institutions." Antisemitism also manifests as the incorrect and ahistorical attribution of the origin of the enslavement of Africans to Jewish people (when in reality it was originated by followers of the Catholic church), or the incorrect attribution of the crucifixion of Jesus Christ, who was himself Jewish, to Jewish people (when it was actually done by the Romans). Many of the millennia-old methods of antisemitic violence and institutionalized anti-Jewish discrimination are used in concert with and inform the social reproduction of racism and white supremacy.

The way we speak and the words we choose are important when discussing and combating antisemitism. Since the term "Jews" has been used pejoratively outside the Jewish community, it is more appropriate for non-Jewish people to say "Jewish people." "Jews" is generally acceptable within the Jewish community, however, so non-Jewish people should take care not to police the language used by people within the community. This is an important lesson to keep in mind because communities are entitled to describe themselves however they like, and non-community members should not attempt to regulate that. It's also important to keep in mind that terminology is not universally approved or rejected by various communities, because within communities there is a vast range of opinions and approval about the use of various terms. The guidance here is specific to the context of historical connotation.

While you may see the word *antisemitism* hyphenated, educators and organizations like the Anti-Defamation League (ADL) and IHRA no longer hyphenate the word. Using the hyphen may incorrectly imply that there is a racial group called Semites. Since 1781, "Semitic" has described a family of languages, but this term should not be applied to a group of people. (Take note, though, that it is accurate to hyphenate "anti-Jewish," since "Jewish" is indeed an identity and community of people.) The ADL succinctly states that antisemitism "is wrapped up in complicated historical, political, religious, and social dynamics." Similar to how "science" was used to support and advance racism, in 1879 Wilhelm Marr invented the term "Antisemitismus" and "anti-Semite" to make hatred of Jewish people sound "scientific" and "legitimate." Simultaneously, Marr incorrectly asserted that Jewish people were a racial group called Semites. Previous to this, the term "Judenhass" was used to mean "hatred of Jewish people." Getting smarter about antisemitism will help us to get smarter about other forms of oppression while making the world safer for Jewish people. This means listening to Jewish people when they speak up about the oppression they face, calling out antisemitism when we see it or hear it, and continuing to recognize and work on unlearning intrapersonal, interpersonal, and institutional anti-Jewish bias and hatred.

RACISM

When Barack Obama became the first Black president of the United States in 2008, the fallacy of a "post-racial" society emerged in popular discourse. This idea incorrectly held that the election of a Black president in the United States meant that racism was no longer a factor in American society. This was, of course, untrue. Getting smarter about racism means understanding that the achievements of individual racialized people do not negate the realities of racism for themselves or their communities. Race and racism have been codified through violence, colonization, imperialism, and genocide for the past six hundred years. Reducing the daily oppression and violence of racism and white supremacy to something that can be undone and resolved by the accomplishments of one or even a handful of racialized people is reductive, and racist itself.

A similar problematic approach is to say you "don't see color" or are "color blind" or "race blind." The idea behind this misguided understanding is that if we "ignore" or just don't focus on race, then race will cease to matter and racism will become obsolete. But race and racism are not the same as having the occasional pimple—these global and ingrained systems of oppression do not go away by leaving them alone. Ignoring the role that race plays in our everyday lives is a privileged position to be in and harmfully erases the lived experiences of racialized people. Race has become so enmeshed in the way we experience the world that it is not possible to simply "not see" it. Not only that, but the terms "color blind" and "race blind" are ableist misnomers—this way of thinking about racism is better described as "racist negligence." Legal definitions of *negligence* describe it as the "failure to use reasonable care, resulting in damage or injury to another," which is apt in the context of racism. Ignoring the harms created and perpetuated by racism will only result in more racism. Statements like "I don't see color" or "I don't see race" actually mean "I refuse to acknowledge the role of race and color, and I choose to willingly participate in racist negligence by ignoring these realities and the associated power dynamics because I have the privilege to do so."

The conversation about racism is a vast and important one. To keep us on track toward a clear understanding, we will examine intrapersonal racism, interpersonal racism, and institutional racism next. Understanding racism in these ways will also allow us to understand that it is not only white people who have the potential to be racist. Crucially, however, that does not mean that everyone can personally *experience* racism—in systems of white supremacy, there is no racism against white people because white people are benefactors of racism. "Reverse racism," or the notion of racism against white people, does not exist. This is because racism exists for the benefit and upliftment of white people. White people may experience other forms of oppression and discrimination like sexism, classism, and ableism, but these will be exacerbated for everyone else because of racism. It's all connected.

INTRAPERSONAL RACISM

Intrapersonal racism consists of the internalized and often unspoken beliefs, assumptions, and understandings about ourselves and others related to race (this is also sometimes called "internalized racism"). Racism is not exclusively a concern of oppressed peoples, and getting smarter about intrapersonal racism requires us to be transparent and honest with ourselves about how we participate in systems of oppression. By as early as three years old, children will have absorbed and learned false conceptions of superiority and inferiority based on race. While toddlers may have little control over how they are socialized and what they are taught to believe, it is our responsibility to unlearn and dismantle these conceptions if we are at all aware of their baselessness. If we claim to approach the human experience with mutual respect and dignity, we cannot leave our internalized racism unchecked and unchallenged. We must scrutinize our intrapersonal racism regardless of our racialized identity, and this is especially important for white people to do. This analysis is not easy, but it is necessary, and is only the beginning. Author of *Me and White Supremacy* Layla F. Saad poignantly says that "anti-racism work that does not break the heart open cannot move people toward meaningful change." While it may be much easier to point out the harm that exists around us, it is far more important to take responsibility for our participation, intentional or otherwise, in that harm. Combating intrapersonal racism is an intimate exercise, with the goal being the betterment of not only ourselves but also those around us.

While it might not be as tangible as other forms of racism, intrapersonal racism enables interpersonal and institutional racism to persist. While in some cases we are held down by oppressive beliefs, in other cases we may prop ourselves up with beliefs and biases that are oppressive to others. Understanding ourselves and other people is a core part of being human, but our existence is made shallow and violent when living in and maintaining a white supremacist culture. False beliefs in superiority and inferiority form a fragile foundation on which to base our lives and sense of self; this is at the core of what author Dr. Robin DiAngelo calls "white fragility," which describes white people's reluctance to examine their own intrapersonal racism as well as defensiveness to participate in discussions about race. White fragility should not be conflated with the racist idea that white people are simply more sensitive than racialized peoples.

Feeling on some level that others are inferior to you—whether or not you are racialized or part of their same racial group—often translates into dehumanization and a willingness to support harmful policies like deportation and criminalization, for example, which materially impact other people's lives. Intrapersonal racism contributes to interpersonal and institutional racism because it is our unchecked biases that help us justify externalized forms of racism and oppression. If somewhere in your mind and heart you believe the lie that Black people have a "greater propensity "to commit crime, that's going to impact how you view and treat all Black people, regardless of whether you are aware of or comfortable with the fact that you feel that way. Once you identify such biases, it is your responsibility to repair and heal them so that you can prevent yourself from perpetuating further harm.

My intrapersonal racism negatively impacted my sense of self during childhood. Though I am now an adult with a strong sense of self and an advanced understanding of critical race theory and the oppression that contributed to my own intrapersonal racism, I'm sure I still have some unresolved work to do. When I was a child, I was ashamed of my hair (despite my parents' best efforts to the contrary). Fortunately, no one at any point in my life came right out and said I should feel bad about my hair because I am a Black girl or because I have curly and coily hair. But it was still a message that was communicated to me in many ways, and I internalized it. When I was in second grade, I was so excited for school picture day, and couldn't wait to dress up in my best clothes and for my mom to send my picture to my grandparents and other relatives. The photography company made disposable combs available for last-minute grooming for our pictures, but none of those combs were made for my hair texture. Because racialized Blackness is equated with things like curly and coily hair texture, I believed that the reason I was excluded from this simple ritual of belonging was my fault and because of my racialized identity. The white woman who was preinspecting students for the use of these last-minute grooming opportunities made it abundantly clear to me that those combs would not work on "Black people's hair." I was already the only person from my community (other than my sister) at my school, and being the only person in my grade who could not run a disposable comb though her hair to get extra prepared for picture day made me hyperaware of my differences. In hindsight, I now recognize that this was the reason why I begged my mother to straighten the front of my hair for every subsequent elementary school picture day—I wanted to fit in and be a part of the group. I wanted to use the combs that were only designed to work on straight hair.

In this and many other ways, white supremacy and intrapersonal racism deny racialized children a sense of belonging and have long-term impacts on self-acceptance and identity. In some cases, the consequences are more dire, such as in the school-to-prison pipeline or the disproportionately harsh disciplinary responses to the same behaviors by racialized students over white students. Today, I absolutely love my hair, but my decision to wear hijab (a religious Islamic headscarf) and cover it is in some part impacted by these childhood experiences. I not only had to form my own self-identity, but also had to do so against the weight of an oppressive system.

Our internalized biases can be separated into those we are aware of, called *explicit stereotypes*, and those we are not aware of, called *implicit stereotypes*. However, it doesn't matter whether or not we believe we are actively reinforcing our biases—what matters is that we are honest enough with ourselves to admit when we have internalized the false beliefs that our society teaches us about race, gender, disability, self, others, and more. Biases are learned and can and must be unlearned. If we cannot be honest with ourselves and take a dispassionate look inward, we will be hard pressed to then work to root out the interpersonal and institutional racism that is far more identifiable and concrete.

INTERPERSONAL RACISM

Interpersonal racism is racism between people. When we think about racism, this is often the type that comes to mind. There are many different forms of interpersonal racism, just like there are many different forms of human interaction. Interpersonal racism doesn't always manifest in explicit violence, though that can be a part of it. Unfortunately, racism can be present in any and all forms of human interaction.

In many cases, interpersonal racism is the way individual people enforce and reproduce the institution of racism by making it their personal mission to racialize other people and perpetuate racism accordingly. There have been countless tragic instances of racialized people doing simple everyday life activities such as going for a jog, sleeping, or coming home from a store that have resulted in deadly violence at the hands of racist police and vigilantes. The intrapersonal racism that consists of our unchecked biases and false beliefs causes us to make racist assumptions regarding the conduct of racialized people. And interpersonal racism places the onus on racialized people to conduct ourselves in a manner that lessens the likelihood of others inflicting their internalized racism in the external realm. Interpersonal racism may be the arena where racism happens, but it is sustained by intrapersonal racism.

Interpersonal racism is so omnipresent in the lives of racialized people that it may be difficult for us to determine the number of racist interactions we experience on a daily basis. Racism does not occur exclusively in flashpoint moments of violence; it is also like a poisonous mist that slowly but consistently kills us. This reality of interpersonal racism is often described as "everyday racism" or "casual racism." Yet these colloquialisms may falsely imply that the severity and dangers of racism should be downplayed. In 1970, Harvard psychiatrist Dr. Chester M. Pierce coined the term *microaggression* to describe the dismissive, insulting, and disrespectful treatment suffered by Black individuals at the hands of non-Black individuals. The term *microaggression* is often misunderstood as racist actions that are minor or inconsequential. However, microaggressions are not small, nor should they be taken lightly. Microaggressions can be better understood as "death by a thousand cuts," which can be detrimental to a person's health, safety, opportunities, livelihood, personhood, and more.

While overt acts of racism—such as physically harming someone because of racist beliefs—are what we most commonly associate with interpersonal racism, there are many forms of this type of racism. Because we exist within oppressive systems, oppressive behaviors are rewarded. Microaggressions have become so ubiquitous that those of us who commit them might not consider their actions to be racist. Getting smarter about racism requires us to remember the philosophy of ubuntu, or humanity toward others. It is our responsibility to be aware of our racist behaviors, impulses, and thoughts, resolve them within ourselves intrapersonally, and take accountability for them and make amends when they affect others interpersonally. The following pages contain examples of some common comments and questions that are rooted in racism, with explanations of why they are racist and should be avoided.

RACIST COMMENTS & QUESTIONS

WHAT NOT TO SAY	WHY IT'S NOT OKAY
"I don't even see you as [racialized identity]."	When we say something like this, not only does it ignore and minimize the identity of the person in question, but it also indicates that in systems of white supremacy, we can only humanize individuals when we separate them from their racialized identity. Sharing our perceptions about someone's racial or ethnic group is never complimentary— it's actually insulting and racist. It's crucial to work on why we might view someone as an "exception" to our racist assumptions instead of evaluating how the assumptions we may hold are racist.
"You must be good at [insert activity stereotypically associated with a racial or ethnic group]."	The fallacy that race has a biological basis has also resulted in the untrue notion that certain racialized groups have particular skills or proclivities for particular activities. The best way to figure out someone's interests and talents is to get to know them personally, not to make assumptions based on their racialized identity.
"You are so articulate/well spoken."	When we act surprised that an individual exceeded our racist assumptions about them, it says more about us than it does about that person's capacity. These harmful statements reveal the racist perception that racialized people are at an "intellectual or cognitive disadvantage" to white people. We should generally compliment people on the substance of their work, not on the method they use or their ability to communicate that work. This may be appropriate in the case of oratory or speech-related actions.

RACIST COMMENTS & QUESTIONS

WHAT NOT TO SAY	WHY IT'S NOT OKAY
"Do you know [other racialized person]?" or "You look just like [other racialized person]."	A major aspect of dehumanization is the failure to recognize that people are individuals and are not connected to every other member of their racialized group. Assuming that all members of a racialized group know each other or look alike is racist. We should be mindful of whether we are making a genuine observation based on what we know to be possible or whether we are making racialized assumptions when commenting on who looks like/may know whom.
"Is that your real [facial or body feature]?"	Remarking on whether or not someone has a body feature that violates your expectations of what a racialized group should look like is racist. We are not entitled to know anything about someone else's hair, facial features, or bodies, so it's not okay to ask for inconsequential information just because we're curious. Other people are not responsible for fulfilling or satisfying our racist assumptions. We are responsible for questioning and identifying our racist assumptions and making a plan to dismantle them.
"What are you?"	This unwelcome question is often heard by people whose external appearance cannot be easily categorized based on popular understandings of racial groups (and, unfortunately, "a human being" never seems to be a satisfactory answer). The question stems from the impulse to racialize or easily and quickly categorize a person by racial group, and strips someone's personhood away from them (which is the goal of racism). We aren't entitled to know the details of someone's racialized identity or ethnic heritage.

CONTINUED

RACIST COMMENTS & QUESTIONS

WHAT NOT TO SAY	WHY IT'S NOT OKAY
"Speak English. This is America [or any other location or country]."	English is not the best, most important, or most commonly spoken language in the world, nor is it the official language of the United States (there isn't one). While it's not uncommon to be frustrated that we may not be able to easily communicate with someone, criticizing them for not speaking English is rooted in imperialism and xenophobia. It's important to examine where this discomfort comes from and work to identify and repair that bias.
"Wow! You have a really strong accent [or anything related to someone's accent or manner of speech]."	There are 6,500 languages in the world, and countless ways to pronounce words and phrases in different accents. Accents may come from regional differences in the way a person's primary language is spoken, or from differences in a person's vocal cords, hearing, or manner of communicating, but none of these differences should be stigmatized or demeaned. Commenting on someone's accent or manner of speech is not only disrespectful, but also can be microaggression. We should all take care to evaluate the negative associations we may make between ways of speaking and things like class, racism, and ableism.
"Where are you *really* from?"	Usually asked as a disbelieving follow-up to a simple "Where are you from?" inquiry, this question does not come from genuine interest in someone's national or cultural origin. It actually comes from the racist inclination to racialize and categorize people according to race. If someone tells you where they are from, believe them. We don't need to know where someone is from unless our job is to check passports or work on the census. Even if this line of questioning is not meant to be offensive, it is a common microaggression that racialized people experience. It's important to learn about people in intentional and authentic ways, accept the personal information they choose to share about their identity without interrogating them, and check our biases along the way.

In getting smarter about interpersonal racism, it's common to reflect on how we may have gotten things wrong in the past, and to want to reach out to people whom we may have said harmful things to and make amends. Since racism creates power dynamics, it's likely that someone we may have harmed didn't speak up about it because they weren't in a position of power to be able to do so, or because our actions violated the basic tenets of a relationship based on mutual respect. This is one reason why it can be uncomfortable to get smarter about racism—we gain greater context and understanding about how we may have failed in the past. While it can be upsetting to know that we've done something harmful, acknowledging harm is not nearly as upsetting as experiencing harm. Learning is a blessing, not a burden, and learning about the ways in which we can stop ourselves from being harmful is a privilege.

If you have hurt someone—as many of us have at some point or another—the best way to demonstrate improvement is to do better. Without accountability and improved action, apologies are just words, and while words do carry meaning, they must be supported by context. (For more on how to apologize, see page 53.) Forgiveness requires trust and must be earned, and repeated violations and harms may cause someone to no longer want to have a relationship with us. Beyond that, just because someone forgives us for hurting them doesn't mean there's no more work to be done. As we work to be anti-racist, we must take responsibility for our own improvement, not make it the responsibility of others. To that end, if you realize while reading this section that you may have done something that was problematic or hurtful to another person, stifle the impulse to immediately reach out to them. Instead, first examine what led you to take that action in the first place and how you can work to prevent similar action in the future. Also consider whether it would cause more harm or distress for you to reach out in an attempt to make amends or if the best course of action for you is to simply do better in the future. It is not the responsibility of the people we have harmed to make us feel better or alleviate our guilt about having hurt them. We must take care not to center our own feelings instead of recognizing the work we must do going forward. Sit with the discomfort that you may have done something racist, and let that discomfort motivate you to avoid further racist behavior in the future.

Many of us have been on the receiving end of interpersonal racism. In many cases, this happens in a context that is either so fleeting or so mired in unequal power dynamics that we are unable to speak up or address the racism at hand. While I am an educator, I still remember that it is not my responsibility to inform every single person who does or says something racist to me how and to what degree they are being racist. In my experience, there is sometimes so much disbelief that a conversation about reconciliation cannot be had because we are not starting from the same understanding, or truth. If we have been harmed, it is not our responsibility to make someone else understand that, especially if they have not demonstrated mutual respect. Racialized people are often expected to forgive and forget singular instances or repeated patterns of racist behavior. This is not only unfair and exhausting, but also reinforces the racist structures themselves. Let's get smarter about some of those racist structures now.

INSTITUTIONAL RACISM

Racism is not limited to our internalized or externalized attitudes, ideas, and beliefs. Nor is it exclusive to interactions between people. Racism is a foundational and systemic part of countless institutions—as well as our broader society—around the world. This institutional racism is not limited to extremist or hate groups like the Ku Klux Klan—it is a deeply ingrained part of everyday life, especially in the United States and other Eurocolonial countries. Institutional racism is the result of the racist power structures created and upheld by society, and was first described in this way in 1967 by critical race theorists and community organizers Kwame Ture and

Charles Hamilton. The consequences of institutional racism (also called systemic racism) can be felt in all spheres of society, including but not limited to education, government, finance, justice, healthcare, religion, housing, and employment. Housing in particular is a good example of institutional racism and how deeply rooted it is in our society.

In the United States, when a neighborhood is predominantly white, it's not because that neighborhood simply didn't attract Black people or other racialized people—it's specifically because of racist housing policies like redlining and Indigenous displacement. *Redlining* is a harmful and racist practice that denies home loans on the basis of race and is responsible not only for segregated neighborhoods but also for the racial wealth gap in America. Between 1934 and 1968, redlining resulted in 98 percent of housing loans going to white families, and only 2 percent going to Black and other racialized families. Homeownership and the ability to accumulate land is directly tied to wealth accumulation; redlining prevented innumerable racialized people (particularly Black people) from being able to access this wealth-building opportunity. Beyond that, the land in question is only available for accumulation because of the violent invasion of the land now known as the United States and the attempted genocide of Indigenous peoples by European colonizers. Since its founding, laws and policies passed and enforced by the United States have resulted in Indigenous Americans being displaced. In 2020, Native American land ownership and stewardship made up less than 2.5 percent of the land in the United States (roughly the size of Minnesota).

Although it was officially banned in 1968, the practice of redlining still continues, and is not just related to housing. During the COVID-19 pandemic, Black- and woman-owned businesses benefited the least from Small Business Administration loans, despite having similar loan application rates as white- and man-owned businesses. In the realm of small business and start-ups, Black-owned small businesses and start-ups on average receive less than 2 percent of venture capitalist funding dollars year over year. These are both illustrations of deep institutional racism, rooted in the fact that the land and resources of the United States were forcibly seized by white people and then parceled out in a racist and unequal manner that favored white people over everyone else. These actions and policies have had far-reaching effects that have shaped the very social fabric of this country. According to the Economic Policy Institute, Black American wealth constitutes just 5 to 7 percent of white American wealth, largely due to racist US federal housing policies over the past century. Today, the average Black family's income is only about 60 percent of the average white family's income. That is not a coincidence or an accident.

In establishing the idea of the American dream, white supremacy in the form of institutional racism was baked in along the way. Celebrated entrepreneurs like William Levitt developed entire communities like Levittown, America's first suburb, exclusively for white Americans. Standard Levittown leases included clauses that stated, "Levittown homes must not be occupied by any person other than members of the Caucasian race." Across the country, in California, my own grandmother's house, which she purchased in 1962, came with an unenforced 1945 deed that prohibited the sale of the house to "Negro, Mongoloid, and Mexican persons." While the Fair Housing Act of 1968 outlawed discrimination in housing, the effects of racist policies like redlining are still felt today, with only 44 percent of Black families owning their homes as of 2020, compared to 73.7 percent of white families, a wider homeownership gap than existed in 1934. Today, home loans are often denied to people based on racist biases and justified through racist institutions like the credit system. The basis of redlining—and the institutional racism still present in housing and society at large—was segregation, which is a core feature of white supremacist nationalism. As explained by performance studies and national security scholar Akeem Omar Ali, "White supremacy has three core values: white people are genetically superior to other people; white people's culture is superior to other cultures; and white people deserve to live in an all-white country." It is the last of these three values that forms the basis for segregation, redlining, and housing discrimination.

Despite largely being denied access to the American dream and the wealth-building opportunity of homeownership, Black Americans created vibrant neighborhoods and communities in cities such as Detroit, Baltimore, New Orleans, Washington, DC, Atlanta, Compton, Oakland, and more. But institutional racism persists even in majority Black cities and neighborhoods. Today, many of these neighborhoods are being dismantled through gentrification, and the Black families that made these areas attractive to neocolonizers or gentrifiers are being displaced. Businesses, grocery stores, department stores, and banks were all less likely to operate in redlined neighborhoods, which fundamentally shaped those neighborhoods in ways that are still felt today. This is a major reason why historically white neighborhoods are more "desirable" than historically Black neighborhoods. A hallmark of gentrification is when a brand-name grocery store is erected in what was previously a "food desert," or an area with traditionally limited access to affordable and nutritious food. Despite the need for grocery stores and other goods and services, it's all too common for companies to only invest in certain neighborhoods when the demographics of those neighborhoods shift toward white people, another manifestation of institutional racism.

REFLECTION QUESTIONS

- Did you know that race is an invented concept? Discuss or journal about how this changes your understanding of race and racism, and how they affect you.

- Did you know that racism manifests in different ways and to different degrees? How might this understanding change your approach to anti-racism? If you were already aware of this, how has it informed your approach to anti-racism?

- Have you expressed interpersonally racist statements, like the ones noted on pages 118–121? If so, what will you do to avoid making these kinds of comments in the future?

- Everyone internalizes racism. How will you address and unlearn your beliefs about yourself and others that are related to race?

- Give an example of each type of racism (intrapersonal, interpersonal, and institutional) that you've witnessed or experienced in your life.

CHAPTER 6

GET SMARTER ABOUT SEX, GENDER, AND SEXUAL ORIENTATION

Sex, gender, and sexual orientation are related but distinct elements of human identity that are important to understand, affirm, and get smarter about. At the most basic level, which we will expand upon later in this chapter, *sex* has to do with someone's sex traits, like their chromosomes before birth and external genitalia at birth; *gender* has to do with someone's innermost concept of self; and *sexual orientation* (also called sexuality) has to do with someone's romantic or sexual attraction (or lack thereof) to other people. For example, my sex is "female," my gender is "woman," and my sexual orientation is "bisexual." These facets of identity can be foundational to who we are as people, but they can't always be concretely defined—who we are often defies categorization and language. As people, while we cannot simply be reduced to these labels, such labels may help us to understand ourselves. People's understanding of and feelings about their own sex, gender, and sexuality can be simple, complicated, or somewhere in between, and can shift over time.

Sex, gender, and sexual orientation are not binary, but unfortunately they are often—and incorrectly—believed to be. *Binary* means "something made of two parts" or "a division into two groups that are considered completely opposite." If sex, gender, and sexual orientation were binary (which they are certainly not), that would mean there are only two sexes (female/male), two genders (woman/man), and two sexual orientations (straight/gay). But that is not the case. In fact, there are many sexes, genders, and sexualities, all of which are real, genuine, and valid. In terms of sex, there is not a binary of "male" and "female," but a kaleidoscope of possible sex trait combinations. In terms of gender, "man" and "woman" are not the only realities—nonbinary and agender people have existed throughout human history. In terms of sexuality, despite what the media and many institutions uphold, there are many ways to love and to be in the world outside of the narrow scope of heterosexuality and cisnormativity.

Mainstream understandings of sex, gender, and sexuality are based on assumptions, and countless errors have been made in the process of forming these assumptions. Relative to all of human history, these assumptions have only existed for a short time. Many people incorrectly assume that being straight, cisgender, and a man or woman is the only way to be human. There are many reasons for this, but essentially they boil down to social construction, which describes the ways that humans organize society to support their assumptions about humanity. But when we consider the fact that a very limited number of people in power have been able to dictate these assumptions, it becomes clear that the organization of society has been based on the assumptions of the few, not the reality of the many.

There are many harmful social constructs around sex, gender, and sexual orientation, most notably cisnormativity, patriarchy, sexism, and heteronormativity. *Cisnormativity* is the social construct that reinforces the idea of a gender binary and centers cisgender experience as the "default" in human life. *Cisgender* is an adjective that means "someone who identifies as the same gender they were assigned at birth," while *transgender* is an adjective that means "someone who does not identify as the gender they were assigned at birth." Cisnormativity incorrectly positions transgender, agender, nonbinary, and gender-nonconforming people as "lesser" and/ or "abnormal," which is harmful and untrue. *Patriarchy* is a form of social organization that places men and fathers in positions of power in family and social structures. Not all societies are patriarchal, nor is patriarchal society the most successful form of social organization, but patriarchy is pervasive in many cultures. The institutions that were created to uplift and uphold patriarchy make it more difficult for people who are not cisgender men to have power. Patriarchy is maintained by *sexism*, which is prejudice, stereotyping, or discrimination against people on the basis of sex and/or gender, and while sexism can hurt anyone, it disproportionately affects women and anyone who is not a cisgender man. *Heteronormativity* is the notion that binary gender individuals must pair themselves with the "opposite gender" in order to form valid connections and relationships, which upholds the idea of a gender binary and delegitimizes LGBTQ+ people and relationships. The social constructs of cisnormativity, patriarchy, sexism, and heteronormativity can be seen in political and governmental policies, social norms, media such as movies and TV shows, interpersonal communications, advertisements, and merchandising (including unnecessarily gendered products like color-coded baby clothes and soaps labeled "for men"), and more.

In learning about and discussing these subjects, it's crucial that we approach them with intention and remember that we don't have to understand another person's experiences or identity in order to respect them. No one should have to justify their existence or reality, nor should anyone have to "prove" they are deserving of respect. Whether due to laws and policies, pseudoscience, or prevailing social attitudes, anyone who exists outside of these narrow views of sex, gender, and sexuality can face grave challenges. In this chapter we'll explore sex beyond the binary, gender throughout history and across societies, and the kaleidoscope of sexuality.

SEX

Like most people, I was incorrectly taught to believe that there are two sexes, that sex is based on bodies and genitalia, and that it is immutable and inherent to our identity. However, sex is far more complicated than we have been led to believe. Biological anthropologist, sociologist, evolutionary geneticist, and critical race scholar Dr. Shay-Akil McLean defines sex as a determination made through the application of socially agreed-upon biological criteria (or sex traits) of genitalia at birth and chromosomal typing before birth. In practice, the genetic testing required to determine a person's chromosomes before birth is both uncommon and expensive. Babies are assigned a sex based primarily (and often exclusively) on what their genitals look like at birth, as observed by the birth attendant (usually a doctor, nurse, or midwife). Sex traits are extremely diverse and complex. While most lessons on sex will point to chromosomes or karyotype pairings like XX for female and XY for male, these are not the only two possibilities. Even as we get smarter about this complex conversation, it is important to remember that much of the language and understanding is still evolving. As science supports these improved understandings, many institutions destructively attempt to fit our understanding of sex into the incorrect and antiquated Eurocolonial binary.

The belief that the physical or biological body is inherent to who we are is a lie that can be traced back to philosophers like Aristotle and Socrates. Similar to the invention of race, the idea of difference in terms of sex and sex traits was not invented as a neutral idea. Sex was assigned a hierarchal value, and in the context of a Aristotelian ideology, this meant that women were "deteriorated" or "degenerated" versions of men. Aristotle's definition of citizenship plainly included "having a penis." The erroneous ideas of these ancient philosophers were codified into religious and legal doctrine, and enforced throughout the world through European colonization from the 1500s to the 1800s. During the nineteenth century, the modern notion of the sex binary became codified through "science." It is important to remember that science is not immune to political influences. For example, racist pseudoscience incorrectly claimed not only that there were biologically distinct races, but also that there were racially distinct sex traits. The size and appearance of sex organs, for example, are still falsely racialized, leading to the fetishization of all racialized peoples.

Sex is not limited to the sex traits of chromosomes, and chromosome pairings are not exclusive to XX and XY. In fact, there are *many* chromosome pairings. Following are the six most commonly occurring chromosome pairings that result in what we may understand as one aspect of sex traits.

- **x:** Occurs in about 1 in 2,000–5,000 people
- **xy:** Commonly understood as male
- **xyy:** Occurs in about 1 in 1,000 people
- **xxxy:** Occurs in about 1 in 18,000–50,000 people
- **xx:** Commonly understood as female
- **xxy:** Occurs in about 1 in 500–1,000 people

In addition to chromosomes, sex traits are also understood as hormones, internal and external genitalia (also called sex organs), and secondary sex characteristics such as breasts and body hair, all of which exist on a spectrum. The hormones estrogen and testosterone are often incorrectly discussed as female and male sex hormones, respectively. In actuality, all humans have varying levels of estrogen, testosterone, and numerous other hormones. Many people (including me!) have genitalia that do not strictly align with what you might see in a medical textbook. This is because there is no uniform look for a vulva, labia, clitoris, scrotum, or penis. Furthermore, the size and appearance of these sex traits can vary widely. Internally, there are testes, ovaries, and ovotestes, all of which can look different for the humans who have them. Furthermore, most humans have varying amounts of body hair and breast tissue (lactation can even occur as necessary across the sex and gender continuum). Our genitalia can be just as diverse as other aspects of human bodies, like noses, eyes, and hands, and we should not erase these differences simply because they don't conform to what Eurocolonialism and white supremacy have deemed valid or "normal."

Intersex is an umbrella term for people whose bodies don't conform to the binary combinations of sex traits. It is important to get smarter about intersex people by understanding that there are many ways in which sex traits present and develop throughout our lives. According to the Intersex Justice Project, there are over thirty different known intersex variations. Intersex children and adolescents are often subjected to medical violence in the form of invasive and unnecessary surgeries that prioritize conforming diverse bodies to an antiquated binary instead of basing care on the health, well-being, and autonomy of intersex people. Without genetic testing, there's no way to know what our chromosomes are, and chromosomes have become an increasingly emphasized aspect of sex traits since the human genome came closer to becoming fully sequenced in 2001.

As Dr. McLean explains, discussions around sex and gender are not rooted in science but in power dynamics. Instead of liberating humanity from antiquated definitions of sex and gender, institutions and individuals continue to force anyone who exists outside of a binary into one that makes less sense as time progresses. We know that transgender, nonbinary, and intersex people (who can be cisgender, nonbinary, and transgender) have and will continue to exist, yet the construct of cisnormativity prevents far too many people from accepting and embracing these truths. Cisnormativity and sex binarism systematically harm everyone. It is important that we understand human variation as simply human variation, not as "anomalies" or "abnormalities," because there is no such thing as a "normal" or "default" human body.

GENDER

Using the McLean-Imani definition developed by Dr. Shay-Akil McLean and myself, gender is an array of mental and behavioral characteristics that relate to, differ from, and go beyond understandings of masculinity, femininity, and neutrality. Importantly, gender is not binary, nor is it the "social expression" of the Eurocolonial sex binary. Gender is an aspect of our personal identities, and as explained by gender nonconforming gender scholar Alok Vaid-Menon, "Gender is not what people look like to other people; it is what we know ourselves to be." This understanding is foundational to the entire conversation about gender. Whether or not someone expresses their gender identity (or has one at all) is up to that individual, not external expectations or mandates. As we work toward a more humanistic, compassionate, and smarter world, we will have to be mindful that it is our responsibility to reconcile any misunderstandings or discomfort we have about other people, not the responsibility of those who exist outside of our own growing understandings to prove their humanity to us.

The gender binary, or the incorrect notion that there are two distinct and opposite genders, is a Eurocolonial invention that prescribes how we should exist, behave, interact, regulate, and organize ourselves. In her foundational text, *The Invention of Women: Making an African Sense of Western Gender Discourse*, gender scholar Dr. Oyèrónkẹ́ Oyěwùmí demonstrates that in precolonial African societies, people were organized by age, not by gender. Many languages, such as Yoruba, were not gendered. Yoruba society did not impose a political or social hierarchy onto people based on sex traits until European colonization forced sex and gender binaries onto the Yoruba peoples through violence, genocide, and enslavement. Even the category of "woman" was only introduced and implemented in African societies through the regimes of European invaders. By establishing a social hierarchy based on "two distinct and opposite sexes" and creating a moral imperative for human beings to consider themselves as two halves of a whole, the colonizers ensured they would have a controlled Indigenous population to enslave and exploit as a labor force. In this way, the gender binary became a very literal way to control the means of production—human reproduction.

In many societies in which gender was used as a form of social organization, it was still not understood as a binary. Gender identities such as Two-Spirit people in various Indigenous North American nations, hijra people across South Asia, and countless other precolonial nonbinary gender identities, still exist today and are working to rebuild and heal from the violence of colonization. Eurocolonial white supremacy defined not only what constituted "human," but also "woman" and "man," and all three definitions are implicitly coded to only include white people and exclude racialized peoples. The gender expressions of Indigenous peoples were regulated through law, policy, and violence via slavery, colonialism, and imperialism. In her book *Black Sexual Politics,* Dr. Patricia Hill Collins discusses the way Black people in the United States have historically been and continue to be policed because of how we do gender. For this reason and the phenomenon that scholar Dr. Moya Bailey names misogynoir, Black women are viewed as inherently masculine, aggressive, and less "desirable" than other racialized women and white women. *Misogynoir* is a portmanteau, a combination of the words *misogyny* ("hatred of women") and *noir* ("black" in French). Misogynoir is perpetuated through media, policy, and law, all of which have become arenas to maintain and enforce white supremacy as it relates to gender.

Despite the historical and current violence inflicted by the gender binary, there are thriving communities and peoples that understand themselves outside of Eurocolonial gender binaries, and even outside of gender itself. Gender has not always existed, and it has not always been binary. Our society must reflect the fact that human beings exist in infinite diversity and infinite combinations, and that this diversity extends to gender identity and expression.

GENDER IDENTITY, ROLES, AND EXPRESSION

In order to make our understanding of gender more concrete, we must get smarter about gender identity, gender roles, and gender expression. Gender is an array of mental and behavioral characteristics that relate to, differentiate from, and go beyond understandings of masculinity, femininity, and neutrality, and *gender identity* is how we perceive or understand our gender, if we have one. (I continue to emphasize that not everyone has a gender identity, because conversations around gender often assume that gender is inherent to what it means to be a human being. This assumption is a result of Eurocolonialism, and is not accurate.) When I was born, my sex was assigned as "female" and my gender was simultaneously assigned as "girl" based on the appearance of my external genitalia at birth. My gender identity is "woman." Since my assigned gender and my gender identity are socially defined as "the same," I am cisgender. (*Cis* means "on this side of.") "Transgender" is an adjective that describes a person who does not identify as the gender they were assigned at birth. (*Trans* means "on or to the other side of.") As a cisgender woman I am harmed by sexism and patriarchy, yet I simultaneously benefit from cisgender privilege because as a cisgender person I am considered normative in society. However, normative does not mean "normal." There is no "default" or "normal" way of being a human.

While many of us may be most familiar with the gender identities of "man," "woman," and even "nonbinary," there are myriad names for countless other gender identities, including genderfluid, genderqueer, bigender, demigender, and more. Even within those broad identities there is no single way to express any given gender identity. When discussing gender identity, it is also important to consider the implications of the language we use. As we covered in chapter 1, according to gender theorist Jeffrey Marsh, terms like "preferences" and "lifestyle choices" have long been used to dismiss and delegitimize LGBTQ+ people. Transphobia and queer antagonism must be addressed when discussing gender identity.

Gender identity, like personal identity, is our truth. If someone identifies as woman, that person is a woman. When we consider our perceptions of others to be more important than their reality, we are not only actively dehumanizing them, but we also run the risk of misgendering them, which is harmful. Justice, equity, diversity, and inclusion educator Kay P. Martinez explains that "misgendering is incorrectly referring to a person's gender by incorrectly assuming their gender identity or using incorrect pronouns." If we keep in mind the approach of mutual respect, or ubuntu, then we will know that it is more important to interact with and honor people on *their* terms, not ours. The goal is for a person's personal identity to be reflected and honored socially, and making assumptions can be disrespectful and detrimental to their sense of self.

Gender roles describe the enforced expectations and assumptions society creates about the behaviors, characteristics, interests, mannerisms, dress codes, morality, and worth of different gender identities. Gender roles are the spoken or unspoken rules about gender that are policed both interpersonally and institutionally. Stereotypical gender roles include unfounded notions, such as women are "maternal" and men are "career oriented." While gender roles are deeply restrictive, many people do find a sense of joy and liberation by participating in aspects of more traditional gender expectations. And that is okay. The real problem with gender roles is how oppressive they can be. Because of gender roles, someone's assigned, perceived, or actual gender can dictate everything from the amount of income they can earn to whether they may face violence, the clothes deemed "acceptable" for them, how their existence is assigned or denied value, and even how they should express themselves, talk, move, and live. Despite seeming like concrete facts of how humanity should operate, gender roles and the expectations associated with them are fluid across time, context, culture, and region.

Gender expression describes the ways that we express (or don't express) our gender identity (if we have one). An incorrect understanding of gender expression maintains that men must express or perform "masculinity," women "femininity," and nonbinary people "neutrality." But in reality, there is no one way to be, perform, or "look like" a man, woman, nonbinary person, or any gender person. If you are a man, you look like a man. If you are a woman, you look like a woman. If you are nonbinary, you look nonbinary. Masculinity, femininity, and neutrality are broad and abstract. Centuries before heeled shoes were transformed into the stiletto and became a symbol of femininity, European noblemen wore heels to appear taller and more important than others as early as the fifteenth century. While Eurocolonial gender expectations and assumptions may lead people to falsely believe that masculinity cannot be expressed with red lipstick and heels, the European rulers responsible for plaguing the world with these definitions of masculinity regularly dressed in what I would consider "full drag," with elaborate makeup, powdered and perfumed wigs, and decorative clothing, with no utility other than looking fancy. Still, when cisgender and white men participate in gender-nonconforming expression, they are praised while genderqueer and racialized people are harmed and disproportionately experience violence. Gender roles, expectations, and assumptions reinforce the gender binary by dictating the forms of gender expression that are deemed valid, acceptable, and respectable.

When breaking down the idea of a gender binary, educators and overly simplistic charts may indicate that gender is a spectrum, and this can be taken as a poetic way of broadly explaining gender. However, understanding the array of gender expressions and identities as plots on a scale—with *man* and *masculine* on one end, *nonbinary* and *neutral* in the middle, and *woman* and *feminine* on the other—can cause many people to assume that nonbinary people exist somewhere "between" man and woman. For some individuals, this may ring true, but for others this can be harmful and untrue. It is important to create space for complexity and nuance, because that is what is so beautiful about the human experience. Instead of thinking of gender as a spectrum with only an x-axis, think of it as a fully dimensional universe with constellations, galaxies, and nebulas representing the people who may share communities or similar methods of self-expression and self-understanding.

SEXUAL ORIENTATION

Sexual orientation is a distinct part of personal identity separate from sex and gender. Also called sexuality, sexual orientation is the part of our personal identity that relates to our physical, sexual, romantic, or emotional attractions to other people. How we understand and form those attractions may inform the way we describe our sexual orientation. For many people, describing, naming, or labeling their sexual orientation can be a helpful way of understanding themselves and finding community. Simultaneously, many people do not name, describe, or label their sexual orientation, and this is also a valid way of understanding themselves. It is important to remember that who we are sometimes goes beyond words and definitions.

As a teenager, I incorrectly thought that heterosexuality (or being straight) was the "default" and that anyone who was not heterosexual had to figure out their sexual orientation and *had* to tell others in their lives about it or risk "living a lie." This was partly because every queer character I saw on television had a very prominent and dramatic coming-out episode and because of the oppressive social construct of heteronormativity. As we discussed earlier, *heteronormativity* is the idea that binary gender individuals must pair themselves with the "opposite gender" in order to form valid connections and relationships. Heteronormativity upholds the idea of a gender binary, positions "opposite gender" (sometimes conflated as the also incorrect idea of opposite sex) or heterosexual relationships as the only acceptable ones, and simultaneously delegitimizes LGBTQ+ people and relationships. Even using the term "straight" to describe sexual orientation is reflective of heteronormativity. In American slang in the 1940s, "straight" simultaneously described someone who was "conventional," "exhibiting no deviation," or "proper," and this is when it was first used as a synonym for heterosexuality. During the 1940s Dr. Alfred Kinsey, Dr. Wardell Pomeroy, and Dr. Clyde Martin also published the Heterosexual-Homosexual Rating Scale, popularly known as the Kinsey Scale, which was used to plot people's sexual orientation on a scale from 0 (exclusively heterosexual) to 6 (exclusively homosexual). While the scale is hailed as an advancement in the understanding of human sexuality (particularly in legitimizing and advancing the revolutionary notion that gay people exist), it has also been used to justify the homophobic policies, laws, and attitudes that still pervade society. Similar to how Eurocolonial definitions dominate understandings of gender and sex, the Kinsey Scale created a literal rubric based solely on the experiences of white American men, with research and analysis conducted by white American men. However groundbreaking it was at the time, the complex nature of human sexuality cannot and should not be understood based entirely on previous sex acts, sex partners, and sexual experiences. Understanding sexual orientation as a binary of straight and gay erases not only bisexuality (or defines bisexuality as being half gay and half straight) and other sexual orientations, but also reinforces the incorrect idea that who we are is based on and determined by the act of sex.

The Kinsey Scale was the first resource I found when I was figuring out whether to come out, and what that would mean for me. Using the people I had crushes on throughout my life in place of "sexual history," I placed myself on the scale as a 4, "predominantly homosexual, but more than incidentally heterosexual," and deduced that I was a lesbian. When I came out to my mother I initially did so as a lesbian, but after talking it through, she suggested that we look up "bisexual," because that might better capture my sexual orientation. Thanks to the *GLAAD Media Reference Guide*, I was able to learn what "bisexual" meant and importantly to see the statement, "bisexuals need not have had equal sexual experience with both men and women; in fact, they need not have had any sexual experience at all to identify as bisexual." That felt right to me, and to this day I describe my sexual orientation as bisexual. I am someone who feels affirmed and encouraged by having a way to describe my sexual orientation, though not everyone does.

There are infinite sexual identities, and infinite ways to describe these identities. As we get smarter about sexual orientation, it is important to learn how to discuss it and what words we use. The word *homosexual* is not a neutral one used to describe people who experience same-gender attraction—in fact, it is an archaic term that should be avoided. There is a history of institutions like the American Psychological Association using "homosexuality" to pathologize same-gender attraction as a (nonexistent) mental disorder and of anti-LGBTQ+ bigots using the term to dehumanize LGBTQ+ people. *Queer* has also been used for homophobic, transphobic, and LGBTQ+ antagonistic purposes, and it still may be used this way, depending on the context. However, "queer" is also increasingly used as a reclaimed slur (which is when a community repurposes a derogatory term into an affirming term) and umbrella identity in place of the LGBTQ+ acronym. There is no consensus on the usage of this term, however, which must be kept in mind—not all LGBTQ+ people identify as queer or feel respected by the use of the term, but it is generally considered acceptable within and when used by the community. Additionally, outdated phrases like "lifestyle choice," "sexual preference," and similar variations should be avoided because these terms incorrectly imply that being anything but heterosexual is less valid, less real, and unworthy of respect.

Depending on our individual contexts, sexual orientation may or may not be a central part of personal identity, including for people who identify on the asexual (ace) spectrum. Heteronormativity often leads people to incorrectly believe that sexual orientation is only a concern of people who are not heterosexual, but heterosexuality is itself a sexual orientation.

LGBTQ+ IDENTITY

The full acronym LGBTQ+ (lesbian, gay, bisexual, transgender, queer, and more) is generally used to refer to a person or group of people who belong to the vast community outside of heteronormative and cisnormative definitions of what it means to love and live. Within the community, LGBTQ+ identities are often referenced as "queer identities," and "LGBTQ+" and "queer" are often used interchangeably (though, as previously mentioned, there is no consensus within the LGBTQ+ community in regard to the term "queer" due to its historical use as a slur). The "and more" plus sign refers to many other identities, such as nonbinary, pansexual, Two-Spirit, intersex, ace, and questioning, which are also part of the community. Sometimes the acronym is written as LGBTQIA+ to specifically include the intersex and ace communities. When the "A" is used in the acronym, note that it definitely does not stand for "allies," because allies (people who support a community but are not part of it) should not be centered in a community they themselves are not part of. However, the perceived ambiguity of the "A" may allow people who are not public about their sexual orientation or gender identity to justify or explain their presence at LGBTQ+ focused events or community spaces.

To get smarter about the LGBTQ+ community, it's crucial to recognize that there is no single way to be within the community and no single way to define the identities that comprise the community. There is an important and necessary variation in the ways that members of the LGBTQ+ community identify. Some people who feel a romantic and sexual attraction to people of two or more genders might identify as bisexual, while others may identify with and add more specificity to the identities of pansexual, polysexual, or omnisexual. The "P" for either polysexual or pansexual is often not included in the LGBTQ+ acronym due to anti-LGBTQ+ individuals and hate groups falsely claiming that pedophiles (predators who sexually abuse children) are an "accepted part" of the celebrated diversity of the LGBTQ+ community. In reality, that is a transphobic and homophobic lie used to stigmatize people who exist outside of cisnormativity and heteronormativity as harmful, dangerous, and abusive.

A hundred lesbians may have a hundred different definitions of what it means to be a lesbian, and that is okay. Some people within the asexual spectrum may experience sexual feelings, while others might not. All these variations of experience and identity are valid. Honoring the diversity of what it means to be human also means honoring the diversity within the ways we understand and describe humanity. Following is an overview of some terms that can serve as a starting point for understanding LGBTQ+ identities. Keep in mind that these identities are not the only or most important parts of the LGBTQ+ community, and that the terms do not universally apply to everyone who belongs to these various communities.

LGBTQ+ TERMINOLOGY

TERM	DEFINITION
Agender	Describes a person who does not have a gender.
Asexual	Describes a person who experiences little to no physical, sexual, romantic, or emotional attraction to other people. "Ace" is used as the abbreviation for asexual, but it's also used as an umbrella term to include "demisexuals" and "greysexuals," who may fall somewhere in between the spectrum of asexuality and allosexuality (the opposite of asexuality), and the definitions may differ from person to person.
Bigender	Describes a person who has two gender identities or a combination of two gender identities.
Bisexual	Describes a person who forms a physical, sexual, romantic, or emotional attraction to two or more genders.
Cisgender	Describes a person whose gender identity is the same as the gender they were assigned at birth.
Demigender	Describes a person who has a partial, but not full, connection to one or more gender identities or to the concept of gender.
Gay	Describes a person who forms a physical, sexual, romantic, or emotional attraction to people of the same gender. "Homosexual" is archaic and offensive due to the history of the word being used to pathologize and malign gay people.
Genderfluid	Describes a person whose gender identity varies over time.

CONTINUED

LGBTQ+ TERMINOLOGY

TERM	DEFINITION
Heterosexual/ Straight	Describes a person who forms a physical, sexual, romantic, or emotional attraction to men if they are a woman and to women if they are a man. Often defined as a person who is "sexually attracted to people of the opposite sex," this conflates sex and gender, which are distinct, and perpetuates the gender binary by claiming that there are two sexes that are "opposite," which is incorrect.
Intersex	An umbrella term for people whose bodies do not conform to the binary combinations of sex traits. Sex traits present and develop throughout our lives, and there are over thirty different known intersex variations.
Lesbian	Describes a woman who forms a physical, sexual, romantic, or emotional attraction to other women. Other definitions define lesbian as "a non-man who forms a physical, sexual, romantic, or emotional attraction to other non-men," though the conversation around gender identity and self-definition in the lesbian community continues.
Nonbinary	Describes an array of gender identities that do not conform to binary gender. Nonbinary gender may relate to, differ from, and go beyond understandings of masculinity, femininity, and neutrality. Nonbinary may be understood within the umbrella of transgender identity, although not all nonbinary people are transgender and not all transgender people are nonbinary.
Omnisexual	Describes a person who forms a physical, sexual, romantic, or emotional attraction to all genders.
Pansexual	Describes a person who forms a physical, sexual, romantic, or emotional attraction to people regardless of gender.
Polysexual	Describes a person who forms a physical, sexual, romantic, or emotional attraction to many genders.

LGBTQ+ TERMINOLOGY

TERM	DEFINITION
Queer	Denoting or relating to a sexual orientation or gender identity that does not correspond to heteronormativity or cisnormativity.
Transgender	Describes a person whose gender identity differs from the gender they were assigned at birth.
Two-Spirit	An umbrella term used by some Indigenous North American nations, traditions, and cultures to describe people who exist outside of cisnormativity and/or heteronormativity and/or colonized definitions of gender and sexuality. Being LGBTQ+ and Indigenous does not automatically define someone as Two-Spirit. (Note that this term should not be used by non-Indigenous people.)

As we work to understand ourselves, we may relate more to an identity or terminology that we previously did not connect to, and vice versa. The understanding and formation of our personal and social identities is constantly in flux. You don't have to identify with any of these terms—you can just be you. Language is always evolving and it's quite possible that one label may suit you and another label might not, and this can change over the course of your life. Names, labels, and descriptions are just words, and as with any word, we use them to communicate a particular idea or experience. Labels help some people conceptualize who they are and can help build a sense of community. That said, gender and sexuality are vastly complex, and you may find that labels are more constrictive than freeing. You don't need a label to validate yourself or your experiences, and you don't need to understand other people's experiences, self-definition, or identities to afford them respect and dignity.

COMING OUT

Coming out is not solely about sharing our LGBTQ+ identities with other people—it is also a journey of self-understanding, self-definition, and self-acceptance. Returning to the concept of personal and social identities, we should remember that who we are in the context of our personal identity (the way we understand ourselves) is legitimate regardless of whether it can be expressed or accepted as part of our social identity (the way others perceive us). While it is a heavily emphasized aspect of LGBTQ+ identity, coming out is not mandatory, necessary, or always possible for everyone within our community. We might come out about our gender identity and later come out about our sexual orientation, or vice versa or not at all. Whether you have previously come out at a younger age or come out later in life, whatever timeline works for you is the appropriate one for you. Importantly, LGBTQ+ people do not have to come out in order to live authentically or to be validly and genuinely LGBTQ+.

Many people and institutions often place the responsibility on LGBTQ+ people to declare our identities instead of disrupting the assumption that everyone is or should be straight or cisgender. No one can tell anyone else how, when, or if they should come out to other people. Coming out is a process, and coming out to yourself is a beautiful experience that no one else can give us or take away. The only perfect coming-out story is the one that happens in our own hearts and minds, because that process is on our own terms. Learning to validate ourselves regardless of the approval and rejection of others is an important gift to give ourselves.

In regard to coming out to other people, media often portrays this as a one-time event, but coming out is not a singular occurrence. I have come out in different contexts and at different times. At fifteen, I came out to my mother. Throughout my life, I have come out to coworkers, classmates, colleagues, friends, family, and partners. Perhaps most prominently, though not most recently, I (inadvertently) came out on a prominent conservative talk show on Fox News in 2017. The day after I came out on national television, I felt extremely vulnerable. Feeling this way is common for many people who come out, particularly if we come out before we planned to, or if we are outed. "Outing" is the harmful and violating circumstance when someone else discloses your identity without your consent. And while every LGBTQ+ person should be able to decide if, when, and how they come out, the unfortunate truth is that this does not always happen on our own terms. Outing is a form of dehumanization and bullying. To avoid outing other people, it is crucial to get smarter about what to do if someone should come out to us.

Back in 2008, when fifteen-year-old me decided that I needed to come out to my mother, it felt like the most earth-shattering experience I would ever endure. I felt pressure from TV shows, movies, and pop culture stories to dramatically declare my truth or risk "living a lie." We must recognize that using phrases like "hiding your truth" or "living a lie" and other euphemisms make malicious assumptions about why someone may not be out, public, or open about their LGBTQ+ identity to other people. Returning home from my high school one afternoon, I asked my mother quite urgently to stop everything she was doing and come into the living room and sit on the couch. I was hoping to set up the ideal coming-out story that I had seen on popular teen dramas. I boldly declared to my bewildered mother, "Mom, I'm a lesbian," and held my breath for her response. She smiled and said, "Honey, you're probably bisexual. You've always formed crushes on girls and boys in your class. Why don't we look up what "bisexual" means, and you can see if it sounds right to you?" My mom has always been LGBTQ+ affirming, and this was apparent in the way she received me when I came out to her. If someone trusts you enough to share a part of themselves with you that you were not previously aware of, that is something that should be considered sacred. One well-intentioned though misguided approach to being on the receiving end of someone coming out includes minimizing the profound nature of what they are sharing with you. Even if you have previously anticipated or assumed someone's sexual orientation or gender identity, it may be inappropriate to disclose this to the person, because it may exacerbate their feelings of vulnerability.

No advice can be universally applied to every instance of coming out. One of the most blatantly harmful ways to respond to someone who has come out to you is to reject them, mock them, dismiss them, or out them to other people. If someone is sharing their innermost reality with us and we reject them, we discard part of their humanity. And while humor can be used to make an uncomfortable situation less so, coming out is a generally serious and profound experience that should be honored as such. Some coming-out situations may be decidedly more light or casual, which is also okay. No matter how someone comes out to you, it's important to respond in a way that feels respectful, affirming, and appropriate to the situation. When in doubt, asking, "How can I best support you in this moment?" is a direct and clear way to determine how to be affirming. Perhaps most importantly, getting smarter about coming out means remembering that any personal information we have been made aware of does not suddenly become ours to share without consent. LGBTQ+ people should be able to come out on our own terms. Follow-up statements like "Thank you for sharing with me," or "I appreciate you being vulnerable with me," and questions like "How do you feel about this?" "Are you out to other people?" and "How can I support you?" are excellent places to begin.

REFLECTION QUESTIONS

- Are sex, gender, and sexual orientation important parts of your identity? Why or why not?
- How does heteronormativity (the incorrect idea that "heterosexual" is the only "valid" sexual orientation) show up in your life?
- Did you know that the gender binary was an invention? If so, when did you learn this? And if not, how does that change your understanding?

- Have you or someone you know experienced coming out? Have you ever been on the receiving end of someone coming out? How have your experiences contrasted with media portrayals?

- Did you learn any new terms in the LGBTQ+ terminology chart? Which ones? Do you have any to add?

- How do gender roles and expectations impact you in your daily life?

- How do you describe your own gender expression? Has it shifted over the course of your life?

CONCLUSION

Congratulations! You've completed another step in the process of getting smarter. I am honored that you have decided to learn with and from me. Throughout this book, we've gotten smarter about history, sociology, key terms, and the context that informs how we understand ourselves, others, and the systems around us. We started with ourselves, examining the role of our personal and social identities. From there we examined our relationships and how they must be built on a foundation of mutual respect, trust, compassion, and consent. To unlearn the harmful lies and replace them with healing truths, we looked outward to the lived experiences, theories, and concepts that shape our society.

Many of the subjects we've learned about overlap and interconnect. Who we are and how we perceive, understand, and treat others has rippling impacts that cannot be understated. Whether in regard to the role of ableism and racism in our institutions, the consequences of gender and sex binaries, or even something as simple as our name, in order to have a more compassionate, informed, and intentional human experience, we need to get smarter. Our lives and experiences have been defined by harmful, archaic, and inaccurate social constructions enforced through European colonization. Assumptions that only work for the few must be replaced with a reality that honors the many. Liberation is not just our freedom from those assumptions, but also the process of identifying ourselves beyond their limited definitions. We cannot simply view liberation as the absence of oppression, but as an entirely new reality that we can bring forth together. Once we attain a smarter understanding, we'll have a better place from which to move forward.

There are many more subjects we can get smarter about, and I hope you will continue your learning journey with joy, curiosity, and the intention to do better. Our journey is far from over. Hopefully, after reading this book you will be equipped with an even wider array of knowledge and tools that will help take you further. Whether you are new to these conversations or building upon your previous knowledge, we can continue building upon these foundations. I hope you continue to get smarter about yourself and the world around you, because we will never be finished learning, and that's a blessing.

BIBLIOGRAPHY

CHAPTER 1

Bailar, Schuyler. "Pronouns." Phone interview by the author. February 16, 2021.

Bjorkman, Bronwyn M. "Singular *They* and the Syntactic Representation of Gender in English." *Glossa: A Journal of General Linguistics* 2, no. 1 (2017): 80.

Brown, Ayanna F., and Janice Tuck Lively. "'Selling the Farm to Buy the Cow': The Narrativized Consequences of 'Black Names' from Within the African American Community." *Journal of Black Studies* 43, no. 6 (2012): 667–92. Accessed December 29, 2020. http://www.jstor.org/stable/23414664.

Carvalho, Jean-Paul. "Identity-Based Organizations." *American Economic Review* 106, no. 5 (2016): 410–14. Accessed December 28, 2020. http://www.jstor.org/stable/43861054.

Fryer, Roland G., Jr., and Steven D. Levitt. "The Causes and Consequences of Distinctively Black Names." *Quarterly Journal of Economics* 119, no. 3 (2004): 767–805.

Goldsworthy, Alison, and Julian L. Huppert. "Bleak Future Ahead." *Horizons: Journal of International Relations and Sustainable Development* 15 (2020): 60–69.

Haviland, William A., Harald E. L. Prins, Bunny McBride, and Dana Walrath. *Cultural Anthropology: The Human Challenge*. 13th ed. Independence, KY: Cengage Learning, 2010.

Imani, Blair. *Making Our Way Home: The Great Migration and the Black American Dream*. Emeryville, CA: Ten Speed Press, 2020.

Kang, Sonia K., Katherine A. DeCelles, András Tilcsik, and Sora Jun. "Whitened Résumés: Race and Self-Presentation in the Labor Market." *Administrative Science Quarterly* 61, no. 3 (2016): 469–502.

Kyzer, Larissa. "Icelandic Names Will No Longer Be Gendered." *Iceland Review*, June 24, 2019. Accessed February 16, 2021. https://www.icelandreview.com/news/icelandic-names-will-no-longer-be-gendered/.

Larson, Carlton F. W. "Naming Baby: The Constitutional Dimensions of Parental Naming Rights." *George Washington Law Review* 80 (2011): 159.

MacNamara, Jessica, Sarah Glann, and Paul Durlak. "Experiencing Misgendered Pronouns: A Classroom Activity to Encourage Empathy." *Teaching Sociology* 45, no. 3 (2017): 269–78. Accessed April 16, 2021. http://www.jstor.org/stable/26429227.

Marsh, Jeffrey. "Pronouns and Personal Identity." Phone interview by the author. January 10, 2021.

Martinez, Kay. "Pronouns 101: Why They Matter and What to Do (and Not Do) If You Misgender Someone." *Medium*, October 7, 2019. Accessed February 16, 2021. https://medium.com/awaken-blog /pronouns-101-why-they-matter-and-what-to-do-and-not-do-if-you -misgender-someone-cfd747c762d1.

Milo. "Naming and Transition." Online interview by the author. December 29, 2020.

Muhammad, Ibrahim Abdullah. "Naming Practices in the Nation of Islam." Phone interview by the author. February 27, 2021.

Neiman, Fraser, and Leslie McFaden. "Current Research at Monticello." *African Diaspora Archaeology Newsletter* 4, no. 2 (1997): 13.

Norris, Stephen P., and Robert H. Ennis. *Evaluating Critical Thinking*. The Practitioners' Guide to Teaching Thinking Series. Pacific Grove, CA: Critical Thinking Press and Software, 1989.

Olson, Eric T. "Personal Identity." *Stanford Encyclopedia of Philosophy*. Stanford University, Spring 2021. https://plato.stanford.edu/archives /spr2021/entries/identity-personal/.

Pilcher, Jane. "Names, Bodies and Identities." *Sociology* 50, no. 4 (2016): 764–79. Accessed December 29, 2020. https://www.jstor.org /stable/26555809.

Sinclair-Palm, Julia. "'It's Non-Existent': Haunting in Trans Youth Narratives about Naming." Occasional Paper Series, no. 37 (2017): 7.

Stets, Jan E., and Peter J. Burke. "Identity Theory and Social Identity Theory." *Social Psychology Quarterly* 63, no. 3 (2000): 224–37. Accessed December 28, 2020. doi:10.2307/2695870.

Suzuki, Mami. "A Long History of Japanese Names." Tofugu. September 10, 2014. Accessed February 16, 2021. https://www.tofugu.com/japan/history-of-japanese-names/.

Túb.osún, K.olá. "Yoruba Names." YorubaName.com. Accessed February 10, 2021. https://www.yorubaname.com/.

Túb.osún, K.olá. "Yoruba Names." Email interview by the author. February 18, 2021.

CHAPTER 2

Battle, Michael. *Ubuntu: I in You and You in Me*. New York: Seabury Books, 2009.

Berscheid, Ellen. "The Greening of Relationship Science." *American Psychologist* 54, no. 4 (1999): 260.

Bloom, Lauren M. *Art of the Apology: How, When, and Why to Give and Accept Apologies*. New York: Fine & Kahn, 2014.

Covington, Stephanie S. *A Woman's Way Through the Twelve Steps*. Center City, MN: Hazelden Publishing, 2009.

Derlega, Valerian J., ed. *Communication, Intimacy, and Close Relationships*. London: Elsevier Science, 2013.

Helm, Bennett. "Friendship." *Stanford Encyclopedia of Philosophy*. (Fall 2017 Edition), edited by Edward N. Zalta. https://plato.stanford.edu/archives/fall2017/entries/friendship.Imani, Blair, Diana Sousa, and Kylie McCauley. "Identifying Abuse." Equality for HER. October 1, 2018. Accessed January 10, 2021. https://equalityforher.com/resources/identifying-abuse/.

Ives-Rublee, Mia. "Transracial Adoption." Phone interview by the author. February 8, 2021.

Johnson Dias, Janice. *Parent Like It Matters: How to Raise Joyful, Change-Making Girls*. New York: Ballantine Books, 2021.

Lim, S., H. I. Yoon, K-H Song, E. S. Kim, and H. B. Kim. "Face Masks and Containment of COVID-19: Experience from South Korea." *Journal of Hospital Infection* 106, no. 1 (September 2020): 206–7. Accessed January 16, 2021. https://www.ncbi.nlm.nih.gov/pmc/articles/PMC7291980/.

Ngomane, Nompumelelo Mungi. *Everyday Ubuntu: Living Better Together, the African Way*. London: Transworld, 2019.

Nkrumah, Kwame. *Consciencism: Philosophy and Ideology for De-colonization and Development with Particular Reference to the African Revolution*. New York: NYU Press, 2009. Accessed December 16, 2020. http://www.jstor.org/stable/j.ctvwrm4jh.

Robb, Alice. "Facebook Didn't Invent the Verb 'Unfriend'." *New Republic*, May 22, 2014. Accessed April 16, 2021. https://newrepublic.com/article/117857/unfriending-facebook-didnt-invent-verb.

Schlagel, Danielle. *Our Modern Blended Family: A Practical Guide to Creating a Happy Home*. Emeryville, CA: Rockridge Press, 2019.

US Health Resources & Services Administration. "Definition of Family." July 26, 2017. Accessed April 16, 2021. https://www.hrsa.gov/get-health-care/affordable/hill-burton/family.html.

Wegar, Katarina. "Adoption, Family Ideology, and Social Stigma: Bias in Community Attitudes, Adoption Research, and Practice." *Family Relations* 49, no. 4 (2000): 363–69.

Williams, Marina. *Surviving the Toxic Family: Taking Yourself Out of the Equation and Taking Your Life Back from Your Dysfunctional Family*. Viale Publishing, 2014.

CHAPTER 3

American Psychological Association. "Definitions of Social Class and Socioeconomic Status." May 2015. Accessed March 10, 2021. https://www.apa.org/pi/ses/resources/class/definitions.

Amin, Samir. *Eurocentrism*. New York: Monthly Review Press, 2009.

Bailey, Moya, and Blair Imani. "Oppression and Empowerment: An Honest Conversation on Intersectionality." Panel presentation, UC San Diego Associated Students Office of External Affairs, February 22, 2021 [virtual].

Bhattacharya, Tithi. "How Not to Skip Class: Social Reproduction of Labor and the Global Working Class." In *Social Reproduction Theory: Remapping Class, Recentering Oppression*, edited by Bhattacharya Tithi, 68–93. London: Pluto Press, 2017. doi:10.2307/j.ctt1vz494j.8.

"Black Women and the Wage Gap." National Partnership for Women & Families, March 18, 2021. https://www.nationalpartnership.org /our-work/resources/economic-justice/fair-pay/african-american -women-wage-gap.pdf.

Boyce Davies, Carole. *Left of Karl Marx: The Political Life of Black Communist Claudia Jones*. Durham, NC: Duke University Press, 2008.

Browne, Jaron. "Rooted in Slavery: Prison Labor Exploitation." *Race, Poverty & the Environment* 17, no. 1 (2010): 78–80.

Burden-Stelly, Charisse. "Race, Class, Racial Capitalism." Online interview by the author. December 25, 2020.

Burden-Stelly, Charisse, and Percy C. Hintzen. "Culturalism, Development, and the Crisis of Socialist Transformation: Identity, the State, and National Formation in Thomas's Theory of Dependence." *The CLR James Journal* 22, no. ½ (2016): 191–214. Accessed April 16, 2021. https://www.jstor.org/stable/26752131.

Collins, Chuck, and Omar Ocampo. "Updates: Billionaire Wealth, U.S. Job Losses and Pandemic Profiteers." Inequality.org, February 25, 2021. Accessed April 16, 2021. https://inequality.org/great-divide /updates-billionaire-pandemic/.

Crenshaw, Kimberlé. "Demarginalizing the Intersection of Race and Sex: A Black Feminist Critique of Antidiscrimination Doctrine, Feminist Theory and Antiracist Politics." *University of Chicago Legal Forum* (1989): 139.

Democracy at Work Institute. "What Is a Worker Cooperative?" Accessed April 15, 2021. https://institute.coop/what-worker-cooperative.

Donner, Francesca, and Emma Goldberg. "In 25 Years, the Pay Gap Has Shrunk by Just 8 Cents." *New York Times*, March 24, 2021. Accessed March 24, 2021. https://www.nytimes.com/2021/03/24/us/equal-pay -day-explainer.html.

Falkinger, Josef. "Skilled and Unskilled Labor." In *Contributions to Economics: A Theory of Employment in Firms*, edited by Werner A. Müller and Martina Bihn. Berlin: Springer-Verlag, 2002. https://doi.org /10.1007/978-3-7908-2649-4_5.

Federal Bureau of Prisons. "UNICOR." Accessed April 14, 2021. https://www.bop.gov/inmates/custody_and_care/unicor_about.jsp.

Gladwell, Malcolm. *Outliers: The Story of Success*. New York: Little, Brown, 2008.

Lal, Priya. *African Socialism in Postcolonial Tanzania: Between the Village and the World*. Cambridge: Cambridge University Press, 2015.

Lean In. "Women Are Paid Less Than Men—and That Hits Harder in an Economic Crisis." Accessed April 30, 2021. https://leanin.org /equal-pay-data-about-the-gender-pay-gap.

Lerner, Michele. "One Home, a Lifetime of Impact." *Washington Post,* July 23, 2020. Accessed April 14, 2021. https://www.washingtonpost .com/business/2020/07/23/black-homeownership-gap/.

Littler, Jo. *Against Meritocracy: Culture, Power and Myths of Mobility*. London: Routledge, 2017.

Marx, Karl, Edward B. Aveling, Ernest Untermann, Samuel Moore, and Friedrich Engels. *Capital: A Critique of Political Economy*. New York: Modern Library, 1906.

McDowell, Robin, and Margie Mason. "Cheap Labor Means Prisons Still Turn a Profit, Even During a Pandemic." PBS. May 8, 2020. Accessed April 13, 2021. https://www.pbs.org/newshour/economy /cheap-labor-means-prisons-still-turn-a-profit-even-during-a-pandemic.

Nash, Jennifer C. *Black Feminism Reimagined: After Intersectionality*. Durham, NC: Duke University Press, 2018.

Nkrumah, Kwame. *Consciencism: Philosophy and Ideology for De-colonization and Development with Particular Reference to the African Revolution*. New York: NYU Press, 2009. Accessed December 16, 2020. http://www.jstor.org/stable/j.ctvwrm4jh.

Robinson, Cedric J. *Black Marxism: The Making of the Black Radical Tradition*. Chapel Hill: University of North Carolina Press, 2005.

Semuels, Alana. "Getting Rid of Bosses." *The Atlantic*, July 14, 2015. Accessed April 16, 2021. https://www.theatlantic.com/business /archive/2015/07/no-bosses-worker-owned-cooperatives/397007/.

SSI Spotlight on Resources. "Understanding SSI." Accessed April 10, 2021. https://www.ssa.gov/ssi/spotlights/spot-resources.htm.

Sweezy, Paul. *The Transition from Feudalism to Capitalism*. London: Verso, 1978.

US Department of Housing and Urban Development (HUD). "2019 Point in Time Estimates of Homelessness in the U.S." Accessed April 10, 2021. https://www.hud.gov/2019-point-in-time-estimates-of-homelessness-in-US.

CHAPTER 4

Barbarin, Imani. "The Ableism That Got Us Here." Online interview by the author. July 3, 2020.

Brown, Keah. "Models of Disability." Phone interview by the author. January 3, 2021.

Centers for Disease Control and Prevention. "Disability and Health Overview." September 16, 2020. Accessed January 16, 2021. https://www.cdc.gov/ncbddd/disabilityandhealth/disability.html.

Charlton, James I. *Nothing About Us Without Us: Disability Oppression and Empowerment*. Berkeley: University of California Press, 2000.

Cokley, Rebecca. "Disability and Ableism." Phone interview by the author. January 22, 2021.

Cokley, Rebecca. "Why 'Special Needs' Is Not Helpful." *Medium*, March 1, 2020. Accessed January 10, 2021. https://rebecca-cokley.medium.com /why-special-needs-is-1959e2a6b0e.

Goering, Sara. "Rethinking Disability: The Social Model of Disability and Chronic Disease." *Current Reviews in Musculoskeletal Medicine* 8, no. 2 (April 2015). Accessed April 16, 2021. https://www.ncbi.nlm.nih.gov /pmc/articles/PMC4596173/.

Imani, Blair. *Modern HERstory: Stories of Women and Nonbinary People Rewriting History*. Emeryville, CA: Ten Speed Press, 2018.

Kapit, Dylan. "Neurodiversity and Autism." Phone interview by the author. February 22, 2021.

Ladau, Emily. *Demystifying Disability: What to Know, What to Say, and How to Be an Ally*. Emeryville, CA: Ten Speed Press, 2021.

Wong, Alice, ed. *Disability Visibility: First-Person Stories from the Twenty-First Century*. New York: Vintage Books, 2020.

CHAPTER 5

Ali, Akeem Omar. "White Supremacy and National Security." In-person interview by the author. January 3, 2021.

Amuleru-Marshall, Omowale. "Political and Economic Implications of Alcohol and Other Drugs in the African-American Community." In *An African-Centered Model of Prevention for African-American Youth at High Risk*. Report No. CASP-TR-6; DHHS-(SMA) 93-2015, 23. Rockville, MD: Substance Abuse and Mental Health Services Administration, 2015.

Bhattacharya, Tithi. "Introduction: Mapping Social Reproduction Theory." *In Social Reproduction Theory: Remapping Class, Recentering Oppression*, edited by Bhattacharya Tithi, 1–20. London: Pluto Press, 2017. Accessed April 16, 2021. doi:10.2307/j.ctt1vz494j.5.

Boen, Courtney. "Death by a Thousand Cuts: Stress Exposure and Black–White Disparities in Physiological Functioning in Late Life." *Journals of Gerontology* Series B 75, no. 9 (2020): 1937–50.

Broeck, Sabine. "When Light Becomes White: Reading Enlightenment Through Jamaica Kincaid's Writing." *Callaloo* 25, no. 3 (2002): 821–43.

Darwin, Charles. *The Descent of Man, and Selection in Relation to Sex*. London: J. Murray, 1871.

Daumeyer, Natalie M., Ivuoma N. Onyeador, Xanni Brown, and Jennifer A. Richeson. "Consequences of Attributing Discrimination to Implicit vs. Explicit Bias." *Journal of Experimental Social Psychology* 84 (2019): 103812.

Disney, A. R. *A History of Portugal and the Portuguese Empire: From Beginnings to 1807*. Cambridge: Cambridge University Press, 2013.

Fuentes, Agustín, Rebecca Rogers Ackermann, Sheela Athreya, Deborah Bolnick, Tina Lasisi, Sang-Hee Lee, Shay-Akil McLean, and Robin Nelson. "AAPA Statement on Race and Racism." *American Journal of Physical Anthropology* 169, no. 3 (2019): 400–402.

Glenn, Evelyn Nakano. *Unequal Freedom: How Race and Gender Shaped American Citizenship and Labor*. Cambridge, MA: Harvard University Press, 2004.

Hawn, Hilary. "Antisemitism." Email interview by the author. February 17, 2021.

Imani, Blair. *Making Our Way Home: The Great Migration and the Black American Dream*. Emeryville, CA: Ten Speed Press, 2020.

International Holocaust Remembrance Alliance. "Working Definition of Antisemitism." Accessed January 10, 2021. https://www .holocaustremembrance.com/resources/working-definitions-charters /working-definition-antisemitism.

Jewish Virtual Library. "Modern Jewish History: The Spanish Expulsion (1492)." Accessed January 10, 2021. https://www.jewishvirtuallibrary.org /the-spanish-expulsion-1492.

Linnaeus, Carl. *Systema Naturae*, 1758. http://resolver.sub.uni-goettingen.de /purl?PPN362053006.

Maryland State Archives. "Blacks before the Law in Colonial Maryland. Chapter III: Freedom or Bondage—The Legislative Record." November 14, 2000. Accessed April 16, 2021. https://msa.maryland.gov/msa/speccol /sc5300/sc5348/html/chap3.html.

McKnight, Utz. *Everyday Practice of Race in America: Ambiguous Privilege*. London: Routledge, 2010.

McLean, Shay-Akil. "Du Bois Meets Darwin." PhD diss., University of Illinois at Urbana-Champaign, 2020.

McLean, Shay-Akil. "Isolation by Distance and the Problem of the 21st Century." (2020).

McLean, Shay-Akil. "Race/ism: A Human Ecological System." Online lecture, Queering Research 2020-21: Racial Justice, Health Justice. January 28, 2021.

McLean, Shay-Akil. "Social Constructions, Historical Grounds."
Practicing Anthropology 42, no. 3 (2020): 40–44.

McLean, Shay-Akil. Email, phone, and online interviews by the author.
December 2020–April 2021.

Meiners, Christoph. *Grundriß der Theorie und Geschichte der schönen
Wissenschaften*. Germany: im Verlage der Meyerschen Buchhandlung, 1787.

Moses, Yolanda T., Joseph L. Jones, and Alan H. Goodman. *Race: Are We
So Different?* London: Wiley, 2019.

Moya-Smith, Simon. "Indigenous Peoples." Phone interview by the
author. November 20, 2020.

Oluo, Ijeoma. "Race." Phone interview by the author. December 17, 2020.

Oyěwùmí, Oyèrónk.é. *The Invention of Women: Making an African
Sense of Western Gender Discourses*. Minneapolis: University of
Minnesota Press, 1997.

Parfitt, Tudor. *Hybrid Hate: Conflations of Antisemitism and Anti-Black
Racism from the Renaissance to the Third Reich*. Oxford, UK: Oxford
University Press, 2020.

Pierce, Chester M., Charles V.Willie, Patricia P.Rieker, Bernard M.
Kramer, and Betram Brown, eds. *Mental Health, Racism and Sexism*.
London, England: Taylor & Francis, 1995.

Roberts, Dorothy E. *Fatal Invention: How Science, Politics, and Big Business
Re-create Race in the Twenty-First Century*. New York: New Press, 2012.

Roosevelt, Franklin Delano. "Transcript of Executive Order 9066: Resulting in the Relocation of Japanese (1942)." February 19, 1942. US National Archives and Records Administration. https://www.ourdocuments.gov/doc.php?flash=false&doc=74&page=transcript.

Rush, Benjamin. "Observations Intended to Favour a Supposition That the Black Color (as It Is Called) of the Negroes Is Derived from the Leprosy." *Transactions of the American Philosophical Society* 4 (1799): 289–97. Accessed December 16, 2020. doi:10.2307/1005108.

Saad, Layla F., *Me and White Supremacy: Combat Racism, Change the World, and Become a Good Ancestor.* Naperville, IL: Sourcebooks, 2020.

Taub, Amanda. "How Australia's Twisted Racial Politics Created Horrific Detention Camps for Immigrants." *Vox*, November 4, 2014. https://www.vox.com/2014/11/4/7138391/australia-racism-immigration-asylum.

Taylor, Michelle B. "Feminism & Race." Phone interview by the author. December 23, 2020.

Thomson, Keith Stewart. "Eleven: The Color of Their Skin." In *Jefferson's Shadow*, 134–42. New Haven, CT: Yale University Press, 2012.

US Census Bureau. "Index of Questions." US Census Bureau— History. Last modified August 27, 2009. https://web.archive.org/web/20090901084138/http://www.census.gov/history/www/through_the_decades/index_of_questions/.

Wolfe, Patrick. "Recuperating Binarism: A Heretical Introduction." *Settler Colonial Studies* 3 (2013): 257–79.

Wolfe, Patrick. *Traces of History: Elementary Structures of Race.* London: Verso Books, 2016.

Zuberi, Tukufu. "Race Review." Phone interview by the author. April 5, 2021.

Zuberi, Tukufu. *Thicker Than Blood: How Racial Statistics Lie.* Minneapolis: University of Minnesota Press, 2001.

CHAPTER 6

Aristotle. "The History of Animals." Translated by D'Arcy Wentworth Thompson. The Internet Classics Archive. http://classics.mit.edu /Aristotle/history_anim.html.

Bailey, Moya. "Misogynoir." Email interview by the author. April 3, 2021.

Beecher, Donald. "Concerning Sex Changes: The Cultural Significance of a Renaissance Medical Polemic." *Sixteenth Century Journal* 36, no. 4 (2005): 991–1016. Accessed April 16, 2021. doi:10.2307/20477588.

Cervini, Eric. *The Deviant's War: The Homosexual vs. the United States of America.* New York: Farrar, Straus and Giroux, 2020.

Cleminson, Richard, and Francisco Vázquez García. "From Sex as Social Status to Biological Sex." In *Hermaphroditism, Medical Science and Sexual Identity in Spain, 1850–1960*, 29–77. Cardiff, UK: University of Wales Press, 2009. Accessed February 16, 2021. http://www.jstor.org/stable /j.ctt9qhdks.6.

Dozono, Tadashi. "Teaching Alternative and Indigenous Gender Systems in World History: A Queer Approach." *History Teacher* 50, no. 3 (2017): 425–47. Accessed January 3, 2021. http://www.jstor.org/stable/44507259.

Faucette, Avory. "Chapter Four: Fucking the Binary for Social Change: Our Radically Queer Agenda." *Counterpoints* 437 (2014): 73–88. Accessed January 3, 2021. http://www.jstor.org/stable/42981932.

Herek, Gregory M. "On Heterosexual Masculinity: Some Psychical Consequences of the Social Construction of Gender and Sexuality." *American Behavioral Scientist* 29, no. 5 (1986): 563–77.

Hill Collins, Patricia. *Black Sexual Politics: African Americans, Gender, and the New Racism*. London: Routledge, 2004.

Intersex Justice Project. "Resources." 2020. https://www.intersexjustice project.org/resources.html.

Lindsey, Linda L. *Gender Roles: A Sociological Perspective*. London: Routledge, 2015.

Martinez, Kay P. "Misgendering." Email interview by the author. April 6, 2021.

McLean, Shay-Akil. "Glossary of Key Terms." *Decolonize ALL the Things*. July 12, 2017. https://decolonizeallthethings.com/learning-tools /glossary-of-key-terms/.

McLean, Shay-Akil. "Issues of Power, Not Bathrooms." Equality for HER. YouTube, March 31, 2017, e https://www.youtube.com /watch?v=gCTQUx3B7-o.

McLean, Shay-Akil. "Sex and Gender." Phone interview by the author. February 5, 2021.

Morrison, Donald. "Aristotle's Definition of Citizenship: A Problem and Some Solutions." *History of Philosophy Quarterly* 16, no. 2 (1999): 143–65. Accessed April 16, 2021. http://www.jstor.org/stable/27744812.

Neiman, Leah. "Ancient Philosophy and Science Concerning Gender and Sex." Phone interview by the author. July 30, 2020.

Oyěwùmí, Oyèrónk.é. *The Invention of Women: Making an African Sense of Western Gender Discourses*. Minneapolis: University of Minnesota Press, 1997.

Smith, Nicholas D. "Plato and Aristotle on the Nature of Women." *Journal of the History of Philosophy* 21, no. 4 (1983): 467–78.

Vaid-Menon, Alok. *Beyond the Gender Binary*. New York: Penguin Workshop, 2020.

Wall, Sean Saifa. "Intersex Understandings." Phone interview by the author. April 5, 2021.

Westbrook, Laurel, and Aliya Saperstein. "New Categories Are Not Enough: Rethinking the Measurement of Sex and Gender in Social Surveys." *Gender and Society* 29, no. 4 (2015): 534–60. Accessed January 3, 2021. http://www.jstor.org/stable/43669994.

ACKNOWLEDGMENTS

Read This to Get Smarter is my third book, and it captures my teaching methodology, which combines concision, personal narrative, history, sociology, critical race theory, intersectionality, and compassion. This book is testimony to my growth as an individual and as an educator. I could not have completed it without the support of my family, friends, and colleagues.

Thank you to my editor, Kaitlin Ketchum, for continuing to provide me with opportunities to be a multi-genre experimental educator, despite the fact that I am a nontraditional author with a tenuous grasp on the rules of grammar.

Thank you to my parents, Mama and Papa Imani, for encouraging me throughout this process, reading countless rough drafts, and allowing me to share your personal stories with my readers. You raised me to be intensely inquisitive and compassionate, and these traits continue to inform my sense of self and my work.

Thank you to my partner and the love of my life, Akeem Omar Ali, for being open to my stream of consciousness and supporting me throughout this process even while working on your own research and dissertation. I am grateful for your presence in my life, from your love and camaraderie to your insights on the mechanics of white supremacy and politics.

Thank you to my best friend, Ren Fernandez-Kim, for making sure that I met deadlines, took dance breaks, drank water, and included anthropological insights. Your friendship has been a consistent blessing, and I am grateful for you.

Thank you to my colleague, friend, and brother Shay-Akil McLean for your commitment to ethics, community, and public scholarship. You have always been open to my invitations for collaboration, and I am grateful. Your work informs the basis of my understanding of sociology, critical race theory, sex, gender, bioethics, and decolonization, and working with you on this book has made me a more mindful and intentional person.

I am grateful to my mentors and advisors Keah Brown (on disability and representation), Michelle Taylor (on gender studies and feminism), Charisse Burden-Stelly (on race and class), Glory Edim (on the entire publishing process), Moya Bailey (on gender, race, and misogynoir), Sean Saifa Wall (on bioethics and intersex justice), Layla F. Saad (on white supremacy and identity), and Sarah Gibson Tuttle (on business). Each of you has generously welcomed me into your life and provided a wealth of support, guidance, wisdom, advice, and reading lists throughout this challenging process.

I would like to thank my team at Ten Speed Press: Kimmy Tejasindhu, Want Chyi, Kelly Booth, Lauren Rosenberg, Dan Myers, Felix Cruz, and Monica Stanton. Each of you contributed to the process of taking this book from an idea into reality. I appreciate each of you for the time and dedication you provided to make this possible.

Thank you to my brilliant agent Emily Tepper, you continue to advocate for me and introduce me to possibilities beyond my wildest dreams, thank you.

Thank you to my tenacious speaking agents, Sean Lawton and Darlene DiFrishia.

Additional gratitude to my dear sisters Chelsea, Marlena, and Nancy, my cherished brothers Brandon and Chris Kenna, supportive aunt Nikki and uncle Chuck, and beloved in-laws Betty and Ibrahim.

Thanks also to Aja Barber, Alexis Androulakis, Andrea Lausell, Cameron Katz, Cami Zea, Christina Basias, Courtney Quinn, Dylan Kapit, Ericka McGriff, Ijeoma Oluo, Imani Barbarin, Janice Johnson Dias, Jennifer C. Nash, June Eric-Udorie, Kate Pinto, Kay P. Martinez, Kimberlé Crenshaw, Kólá Túbòsún, Lauren Melissa Ellzey, LeVar Burton, Leah Neiman, Maggie Giles, Mandi Dorrell, Mari Ortega, Mia Ives-Rublee, Rebecca Cokley, Schuyler Bailar, Simon Moya-Smith, Victoria Abraham, and Zahra Wakilzada. Thank you to all of my wonderful smarties for getting smarter with me every day.

ABOUT THE AUTHOR

Blair Imani is a critically acclaimed historian, author, educator, and influencer living at the intersections of Black, bisexual, and Muslim identity. The *New York Times* has praised her unique ability to create "progressive lessons with vibrant visuals and a perky, quirky delivery." She is the author of *Making Our Way Home: The Great Migration and the Black American Dream* (2020) and *Modern HERstory: Stories of Women and Nonbinary People Rewriting History* (2018). Her work centers women and girls, global Black communities, and the LGBTQ+ community. As an influencer and historian, semiretired organizer, and public speaker, Blair is dedicated to making the world a better place and amplifying the voices and work of those fighting the good fight. Learn more about her by visiting blairimani .com and following her on social media @blairimani.

INDEX

genderfluid, defining, 143
gender identity, 16, 17, 133, 135–36
gender roles, 136–37, 149
gentrification, 125
given names, 5
government names, 5
Gregorian calendar, 97–98
Gregory XIII, Pope, 97–98
Guardian Appreciation Day, 29–30

H

Hamilton, Charles, 123
"handicapped," usage of, 86
Hawking, Stephen, 81
Hawn, Hilary, 109
hearing disabilities, 89
heteronormativity, 43, 129, 138–39, 141, 142, 148
heterosexuality, 138, 139, 141, 144
holidays, 22
Holocaust, 105, 109
homophobia, 35, 43, 140
"homosexuality," usage of, 140
housing, 67, 123–25
Hume, David, 107

I

identity
  components of, 3, 4
  flower with petals metaphor for, 4
  personal, 3–4, 16, 18, 136
  social, 3–4, 6
  validity of, 5
  See also beliefs; gender identity; names; pronouns; values
identity-first language (IFL), 84–85
illnesses, chronic, 88

Immigration Act of 1924, 104
income inequality, 61–62
Indigenous peoples, 99, 100, 123, 133–34
individualism, 81
International Holocaust Remembrance Alliance (IHRA), 109, 110
intersectionality
  defining, 61
  disability and, 82–83
  labor and, 61–62
intersex people, 132, 141, 144
intimate partnerships
  abusive, 44–46
  defining, 40, 41, 43–44
  labels for, 41
  types of, 42–43
Islam, misconceptions about, 22–23

J

Jefferson, Thomas, 21
Jesus Christ, 110
Jewish people, 100, 105, 108–11
Jones, Claudia, 58, 99

K

Kant, Immanuel, 107
Kinsey, Alfred, 139
Kinsey Scale, 139–40
Ku Klux Klan, 122

L

labor
  class and, 59–64
  classification of, by skill level, 60–61, 76
  defining, 76
  intersectional perspective on, 61–62
  prison, 66–67

See also capitalism; socialism
Ladau, Emily, 77
last names, 12–16
learning, as journey, 1, 152
learning disabilities. *See* cognitive disabilities
Leclerc, Georges-Louis, 101
lesbians, 142, 144
Levitt, William, 124
Levittown, 124
LGBTQ+ people
  coming out, 146–48, 149
  defining, 141
  diversity of, 141–42
  language and, 140–41, 143–45
  toxic family relationships and, 34, 35
  liberation, 151–52
Linnaeus, Carl, 101, 108
Locke, Thomas, 107
Louis XIV, King, 101

M

Malcolm X, 15
Marr, Wilhelm, 111
marriage, 43–44
Marsh, Jeffrey, 18, 136
Martin, Clyde, 139
Martinez, Kay P., 136
McKnight, Utz, 95
McLean, Shay-Akil, 98, 130, 132, 133
Meiners, Christoph, 101–2, 108
meritocracy, 59
microaggressions, 117
middle names, 12–13
misgendering, 136
misogynoir, 134
mobility disabilities, 89

ALSO BY BLAIR IMANI

MODERN HERSTORY: STORIES OF WOMEN AND NONBINARY PEOPLE REWRITING HISTORY

An inspiring and radical celebration of 70 women, girls, and nonbinary people who have changed—and are still changing—the world, from the Civil Rights Movement and Stonewall riots through Black Lives Matter and beyond.

$17.99 | Hardcover | ISBN 978-0-399-58223-3

MAKING OUR WAY HOME: THE GREAT MIGRATION AND THE BLACK AMERICAN DREAM

A powerful illustrated history of the Great Migration and its sweeping impact on Black and American culture, from Reconstruction to the rise of hip hop.

$18.99 | Hardcover | ISBN 978-1-9848-5692-0

Available from Ten Speed Press wherever books are sold.
www.tenspeed.com